BLUEPRINTS

Science 5-7
Teacher's Resource Book

Jim Fitzsimmons

Rhona Whiteford

Stanley Thornes (Publishers) Ltd

First published in 1990 by
Stanley Thornes (Publishers) Ltd
Old Station Drive
Leckhampton
CHELTENHAM GL53 0DN

British Library Cataloguing in Publication Data

Fitzsimmons, Jim
    Science 5–7: teachers resource. – (Blueprints).
    1. Mathematics. Curriculum subjects. Primary schools.
Teaching
    I. Title   II. Whiteford, Rhona   III. Series
    372.7044

ISBN 0–7487–0430–2

Typeset by Tech-Set, Gateshead, Tyne & Wear.
Printed and bound in Great Britain at The Bath Press, Avon.

CONTENTS

INTRODUCTION

What is *Blueprints: Science?*

Blueprints: Science is a practical teachers' resource specifically written to fulfil all the requirements of the National Curriculum in science for primary schools. It is intended for all teachers, particularly non-science specialists, and provides comprehensive coverage in an easy-to-follow format. *Blueprints: Science* is a rich resource of practical ideas to use alongside other materials within your scheme of work. It gives children meaningful, relevant things to do. *Blueprints: Science 5–7* provides activities for Key Stage 1. *Blueprints: Science 7–11* includes activities for Key Stage 2. For each Key Stage there is a Teacher's Resource Book and a book of Pupils' Copymasters.

Blueprints and the National Curriculum

This Teacher's Resource Book and the accompanying Pupils' Copymaster Book closely follow the structure of the publication *Science in the National Curriculum* (HMSO, 1989). The Teacher's Resource Book is arranged in sections, each corresponding to work at a Level of the National Curriculum. In addition, on page vii, there is a Programme of Study Planner which enables you to use the activities across Levels to resource the Programme of Study for Key Stage 1. The Pupils' Copymasters reinforce and extend the activities in this book.

Blueprints and topics

Blueprints: Science is a flexible resource and can be used in subject lessons devoted exclusively to the learning of science or in the learning of scientific principles while doing topic work. On pages viii–x of this Teacher's Resource Book is a Topic Planner chart which lists many of the topics in common use. Alongside each topic title is an indicator to show at which Levels and in which Attainment Targets (ATs) there is work which can easily make a contribution to the topic.

Blueprints Science 5–7

This Teacher's Resource Book provides dozens of practical explorations and activities through Key Stage 1. The book is arranged in three sections. The sections relate to work expected of children through this Key Stage, i.e. Levels 1, 2 and 3. This is the span of attainment that children are expected to achieve by the end of Key Stage 1. Most children are expected to have reached Level 2; only some are likely to be naturally into Level 3. For this reason the emphasis on activities in this book is on Levels 1 and 2. The Level 3 section is shorter and provides outline activities for the more advanced children. Within each section of the book the heading for work in each Attainment Target

is a reproduced extract from the Statutory Provisions, comprising the AT title and applicable Statements of Attainment:

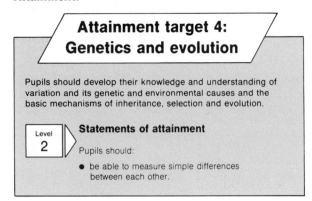

Attainment target 4: Genetics and evolution

Pupils should develop their knowledge and understanding of variation and its genetic and environmental causes and the basic mechanisms of inheritance, selection and evolution.

Level 2	**Statements of attainment**
	Pupils should:
	• be able to measure simple differences between each other.

This Teacher's Resource Book will prove an invaluable resource, even without the use of the Pupils' Copymasters. You can, in developing your own schemes of work, consult the *National Curriculum Key Stage 1 Programme of Study* and choose activities to fit those elements on which you are focusing. The coverage of the activities is comprehensive and, as far as possible, the use of secondary sources has been avoided. The symbol ⚠ has been included to denote safety advice where this is considered to be beneficial. There are record sheets at the back, on which you can identify activities you and the children have tried, and also note work done which contributes to AT1.

The Pupils' Copymaster Book provides 91 photocopiable worksheets linked to many of the activities in this Teacher's Resource Book. The worksheets reinforce and extend activities already done and provide opportunities to record activities and results in an organised way. When completed, the worksheets can be added to children's workfiles or used as exemplar material in pupil profiles. They may also be seen as a resource for teacher assessment. There are record sheets at the back, on which you can note the copymasters the children have made use of, and their experience of work contributing to AT1.

Attainment Targets 2–6 and 9–16

Across all these ATs *Blueprints: Science 5–7* provides coverage of Levels 1–3. It is expected that most children should master Level 2 but Level 3 work is provided for those children who require work beyond Level 2. In line with the overall balance of the book, the Copymaster Book provides three activities per level of Attainment Target for Levels 1 and 2, and one activity at Level 3.

Attainment Target 1

Attainment Target 1, The exploration of science, has been treated differently from the other ATs. It comprises half the science curriculum at Key Stage 1, and is about 'becoming a scientist', i.e. it concentrates on the methods of scientific enquiry, rather than substantive knowledge. We have chosen to use the activities in all the other ATs as vehicles for the acquisition of skills in AT1. At the beginning of the work at each Level, you will find a brief summary of how you should incorporate work on AT1 into the activities. Symbols have been created to show how we envisage work on copymasters will also contribute to an understanding of AT1, and these appear on the copymasters and at the appropriate places in the text of this book. At the start of work at each Level in this book, you will find these symbols explained.

Record keeping

There are three photocopiable record sheets at the back of this book and the Pupils' Copymaster Book. The first two cover the different levels of AT1, the third ATs 2–16. We suggest you use these as follows.

Teacher's Resource Record Sheets 1 and 2: Photocopy one per child and record how many experiences relating to each aspect of AT1 each child has had. This is a matter for your own judgement. Some activities enable work on many aspects of AT1, others few. The kinds of enquiry the children can undertake will depend also on how you set up the activities. A completed Sheet 1 may look like this:

RECORD SHEET 1: AT1

Key Stage One AT1
Levels one & two

Name Jane Brown   **Year/Class** 2/3

A record of the number of experiences of AT1 processes.

👁	🗣	?	🔍	✏	▦	📖	💡
✓✓	✓✓	✓	✓	✓	✓	✓	✓
✓✓	✓✓	✓	✓	✓	✓	✓	✓
✓✓	✓✓	✓	✓	✓	✓	✓	✓
✓✓	✓✓	✓	✓	✓	✓	✓	✓
✓✓	✓✓	✓	✓	✓	✓	✓	✓
✓	✓✓	✓	✓	✓	✓	✓	
✓	✓✓	✓	✓	✓	✓	✓	
✓	✓✓	✓	✓	✓	✓		
✓	✓✓	✓	✓	✓	✓		
✓	✓✓				✓		
✓	✓						
✓	✓						

Comments
Although Jane has had plenty of experience of discussion she is still unable to join in effectively and take turns. However, she tries hard and continued experience and adult guidance should help.

Sheet 3: Photocopy one per child and record which Levels of the appropriate ATs the children have worked at. There are three columns which you can shade in or put a tick in. They can be labelled thus:

a introduced to . . .
b has difficulty/needs more work on . . .
c understood . . .

A completed Sheet 3 may look like this:

RECORD SHEET 3: ATs 2–6, 9–16

Key Stage One

Name John Smith

Level ONE   **Year/Class** 2

AT	Area of Study 1			Area of Study 2			Area of Study 3		
	a	b	c	a	b	c	a	b	c
2	✓			✓			✓		
3	✓			✓			✓		
4	✓			✓			✓		
5			✓			✓			✓
6			✓			✓			✓
9			✓			✓			✓
10			✓			✓			✓
11		✓		✓				✓	
12	✓			✓			✓		
13	✓			✓			✓		
14			✓			✓			✓
15		✓		✓				✓	
16		✓		✓			✓		

Comments
Coped very well with ATs 2–4 which he could relate to personally, but had considerable difficulty with the manipulative skills required in the ATs covering physical science, e.g. 9, 10 + 14.

Pupils' Copymaster Record Sheets 1 and 2: Photocopy one per child and put a tick against those aspects of AT1 which, in your judgement, the child has experienced in work they have recorded on the copymasters. There is a bar code containing the symbols we consider appropriate at the bottom of each copymaster to help you.

Sheet 3: Photocopy one per child and list the copymasters each child has worked on. The three columns could be used as suggested above, that is:

a introduced to . . .
b has difficulty/needs more work on . . .
c understood . . .

HOW TO USE THIS BOOK

If you have only the Teacher's Resource Book
You can use this book as a flexible resource which you can consult for ideas, activities and investigations to work on with children.

To use in class:
1 Consult the appropriate part of the Programme of Study in the HMSO publication.
2 Identify the substantive ATs to be studied and the appropriate Levels. Use the Programme of Study Planner to help you. Consult the introductions to the Levels to establish the work to include on AT1.
3 Within the chosen Levels of the ATs, look at the Areas of Study and choose those that will fit in with your work plans for the children.
4 Within the chosen Areas of Study select activities which best fit your management plans and resourcing.
5 Assemble the equipment which you and the children need to carry out the activities.

6 As each activity is completed use Record Sheets 1, 2 and 3 to record what the children have done.

If you also have the Pupils' Copymasters
7 Identify the appropriate copymasters and ensure that you have enough copies. You will find notes on how to use the sheets in this book. You will find the related sheets referred to in this book with this symbol:

Give them to the children at the optimal time for them to do the necessary extension work or recording.

8 Use Record Sheets 1, 2 and 3 to record what the children have done on the copymasters.

This planner enables you to use the activities in this book across Levels to resource the Programme of Study for Key Stage 1 of *Science in the National Curriculum*. For quick reference we have extracted, in shorthand form, the substance of the Programme of Study for each Attainment Target, statement by statement. You will find these statements written out in full in your copy of *Science in the National Curriculum*. Against each statement you will find the place in this book, referenced by page number and Area of Study number (A/S), where that part of the Programme of Study is covered.

AT2 The variety of life
● Find out about a variety of animal and plant life *pp2–4 A/S 1–3, p6 A/S 3, pp33–4 A/S 2, pp36–9 A/S 1–3, pp90–1 A/S 1–3*
● Take responsibility for the care of living things *pp2–3 A/S 1–2, pp38–9 A/S 3*

AT3 Processes of life
● Find out about themselves, how they grow, feed and move, the senses, stages of development *pp4–6 A/S 1–2, pp39–42 A/S 1, pp44–5 A/S 3, pp92–4 A/S 1*
● Keeping healthy through exercise and personal safety *pp43–5 A/S 2–3*
● The role of drugs as medicines *pp44–5 A/S 3*

AT4 Genetics and evolution
● Similarities/differences between ourselves and others *pp7–9 A/S 1–3, pp45–9 A/S 1–3*
● The variety of other life-forms, including extinct ones *pp94–5 A/S 1–2*

AT5 Human influences on the Earth
● Investigate how everyday waste products decay, and keep records *pp9–11 A/S 1–3, pp49–52 A/S 1–3, pp96–7 A/S 1*
● Help improve appearance of local environment *pp9–10 A/S 1–2, p97 A/S 2*

AT6 Types and uses of materials
● Collect, find similarities/differences in everyday materials *p11–14 A/S 1–3, pp54–5 A/S 1–2, pp97–9 A/S 1–2*
● Work with/change materials by dissolving, squashing, pouring, etc. *pp11–14 A/S 1–3, pp55–7 A/S 3, pp55–7 A/S 3, pp97–8 A/S 1*

AT9 Earth and atmosphere
● Collect, find differences/similarities in natural materials (including rocks and soil) *pp62–3 A/S 3, pp99–102 A/S 1, 3*

● Observe/record weather changes *pp15–16 A/S 1–3, pp57–62 A/S 1–2, p10 A/S 2*

AT10 Forces
● Experience forces (push, pull, move, stop, etc.) *pp17–20 A/S 1–3, pp63–6 A/S 1–3, pp102–3 A/S 1–2*

AT11 Electricity and magnetism
● Be aware of uses/dangers of electricity in the classroom *pp20–2 A/S 1–3, p71 A/S 3*
● Investigate magnetic materials and their effects on materials *pp67–70 A/S 1–2*
● Simple activities using bulbs, buzzers, batteries, wires *pp104–5 A/S 1–2*

AT12 The scientific aspects of information technology
● Use information sources and computers *pp23–5 A/S 1–3, pp72–5 A/S 1–3, pp106–7 A/S 1–2*
● Use tape recorders and television *pp23–4 A/S 1–2, pp72–5 A/S 1, 3, p106 A/S 1*

AT13 Energy
● Consider and talk about foods they eat: what, why and when *pp25–6 A/S 1–3*
● Experience of devices which move/store energy *pp77–9 A/S 2–3, p108 A/S 2–3*
● The role of heating/cooling in bringing about melting/solidifying *pp55–7 A/S 3*
● Link hot and cold with temperature measured by thermometer *pp75–7 A/S 1, pp107–8 A/S 1*

AT 14 Sound and music
● Experience the range of sound, find out causes and uses *pp27–9 A/S 1–3, pp80–3 A/S 1–3, pp109–10 A/S 1–2*
● Investigate ways of making/experiencing sounds by vocalising, striking, etc. *pp27–9 A/S 1–2, pp82–3 A/S 3, pp109–10 A/S 1*
● Explore ways of sorting sounds and instruments *pp27–9 A/S 1–3, pp82–3 A/S 3*

AT15 Using light and electromagnetic radiation
● Explore variety of light sources and effects (shadow, reflection, colour) *pp30–2 A/S 1–3, pp83–6 A/S 1–3, pp111–13 A/S 1–2*

AT16 The Earth in space
● Observe seasonal changes (day length, weather, changes in plants/animals) *pp32–4 A/S 1–2, p88 A/S 3, pp90–1 A/S 1, p114 A/S 2*
● Observe length of day, position of Sun and Moon *p34 A/S 3, pp87–8 A/S 1–3, p114 A/S 2*
● Investigate the use of a sundial *pp113–14 A/S 1*

TOPIC PLANNER

If you wish to include science in your topic work look down the following list of 20 common topic titles and identify any that are close to the topic that you are planning. Alongside the title we have indicated, by attainment target, the location of activities in this book which support that topic. Depending on the emphasis within the work you are planning you may be able to incorporate activities in ATs and at Levels other than those we have drawn attention to.

| Topic Title | Levels | \multicolumn{13}{c}{Attainment Targets} | Related Topics |
		2	3	4	5	6	9	10	11	12	13	14	15	16	
Myself	1	●	●	●	●						●				My Family, Pets, Change, Growth, Food, Homes, Clothes — Transport
	2	●	●	●	●						●				
	3	●	●		●										
My Family	1	●		●	●				●						Myself, Pets, Change, Growth, Food, Homes, Clothes — Transport
	2	●	●	●	●				●						
	3	●	●		●				●						
Pets	1	●													Growth, Change, Food, Weather, Colour and Shape, Underground — Homes, Seasons, Time
	2	●	●												
	3	●	●												
Change	1			●	●	●	●	●			●		●	●	Myself, My Family, Pets, Growth, Food and Farming, Weather, Water — Homes, Colour and Shape, Transport, Underground, Building, Time, Seasons
	2			●	●	●	●	●			●		●	●	
	3														
Food and Farming	1		●		●		●	●			●			●	Weather, Change, Growth, Light, Time, Seasons, Underground, Transport
	2	●	●		●		●							●	
	3	●	●		●		●							●	
Weather	1						●	●	●				●	●	Water, Growth, Change, Colour and Shape, Food, Clothes — Time, Seasons
	2	●					●		●		●		●	●	
	3	●					●	●	●		●			●	
Water	1	●			●		●						●		Change, Growth, Food and Farming, Underground, Transport
	2	●			●		●								
	3	●			●		●	●							

Topic planner

Topic Title	Levels	2	3	4	5	6	9	10	11	12	13	14	15	16	Related Topics
								Attainment Targets							
Homes	1				●				●	●	●		●	●	Myself My Family Pets Colour and Shape Building
	2	●	●			●	●		●	●	●		●	●	
	3	●	●		●	●			●	●	●		●		
Clothes	1			●		●	●							●	Myself My Family Change Growth Colour and Shape Seasons
	2	●	●	●		●					●			●	
	3	●				●									
Colour and Shape	1	●	●	●		●	●	●					●		Change Weather Food Clothes Seasons Light
	2		●	●		●	●	●					●		
	3					●	●	●							
Light	1						●			●	●		●	●	Colour and Shape Seasons Space
	2	●	●				●			●	●		●	●	
	3	●								●			●	●	
Transport	1				●			●							Weather Water Underground Space Building
	2				●			●	●		●			●	
	3				●			●			●				
Underground	1	●	●		●										Pets Food and Farming Homes Transport
	2	●			●										
	3	●	●	●	●	●	●					●			
Building	1					●	●			●					Transport Homes Change
	2	●	●			●	●			●	●		●		
	3	●				●	●		●	●					
Time	1									●				●	Myself My Family Change Growth Weather Transport Communications Music and Sound
	2		●		●		●			●				●	
	3	●	●		●					●				●	
Seasons	1						●							●	Change Growth Food and Farming Weather Colour and Shape
	2						●				●			●	
	3						●				●			●	

Topic Title	Levels	Attainment Targets													Related Topics
		2	3	4	5	6	9	10	11	12	13	14	15	16	
Dinosaurs	1														Underground Change
	2														
	3			●											
Space	1								●					●	Transport Light Time Seasons Communications
	2								●					●	
	3								●					●	
Communications	1								●	●					Space Music and Sound Time
	2								●	●					
	3								●	●					
Music and Sound	1								●			●			Communications
	2								●			●			
	3								●			●			

LEVEL 1

Attainment target 1: Exploration of science

Pupils should develop the intellectual and practical skills that allow them to explore the world of science and to develop a fuller understanding of scientific phenomena and the procedures of scientific exploration and investigation. This work should take place in the context of activities that require a progressively more systematic and quantified approach, which draws upon an increasing knowledge and understanding of science. The activities should encourage the ability to:

i.   plan, hypothesise and predict
ii. design and carry out investigations
iii. interpret results and findings
iv. draw inferences
v.   communicate exploratory tasks and experiments.

Level 1

Statements of attainment

Pupils should:

- observe familiar materials and events in their immediate environment, at first hand, using their senses.
- describe and communicate their observations, ideally through talking in groups or by other means, within their class.

As the children are working on activities at this Level they will have the opportunity to do work contributing to AT1 as the activities in the text are all designed to do this. For example, in AT3 (Processes of life), Area of Study 1, Activity 1, the children can be introduced to the different parts of the body through the medium of poems and rhymes and simple games such as 'Simon Says', thus satisfying the requirements of AT1 (Observation and discussion).

A bar code of symbols relating to AT1 has been created and this is the key to it:

Observation   Discussion

The full bar code appears on the record sheet to help you record the children's experiences. These symbols, which are linked to work on the copymasters, appear in the text at the appropriate place.

Attainment target 2: The variety of life

Pupils should develop their knowledge and understanding of the diversity and classification of past and present life-forms, and of their relationships, energy flows, cycles of matter and human influences within ecosystems.

Level 1

Statements of attainment

Pupils should:

- know that there is a wide variety of living things, which includes human beings.

Area of study 1

LIVING AND NON-LIVING THINGS

 C1

Purpose
To introduce to the children the idea that the world is composed of living and non-living things.

Materials needed
As large a collection of objects as space will allow, in these three categories: plants, animals and inanimate things. (The latter can include a variety of natural and man-made objects.)

When introducing any animals into the classroom, do make sure that they are safe to handle, non-toxic and housed and cared for properly. (See DES and RSPCA regulations and guidelines on keeping animals in school.)

Activity
Display all the objects. Where possible allow the children to handle them and explore their characteristics for themselves. Discuss in small groups or as a class, on as many occasions as is practical, the similarities and differences and the children's general impressions and feelings.

With very young children it is important to characterise animals as those which can move, which need food, water and care and which if injured feel pain and possibly die. These discussions of life and death can become part of your RE work. To enhance such discussions it may be possible to invite in a parent with a newborn baby. The children can also be asked to bring in photos of themselves or siblings as babies.

Integral to your discussions about living and non-living things will be the question of favourite toys, which are very much alive to their young owners. The whole question of real and make-believe is an ongoing one for children. Their ideas will develop over many years. It is only with patience and examples and discussions over a long period of time that the distinction between living and non-living, real and pretend can be finally understood. Level 1 of this AT can be seen as the start of this process.

Sort your collection into sets of living and non-living things and label accordingly. Don't at this stage go too far into distinctions about once living things such as wood and fossils, although you can identify the materials. Do make it clear that humans belong to the set of living things. To illustrate this you can do a class self-portrait as part of the collection of things.

Copymasters
Use copymaster 1 (Living and non-living) as a sorting and classifying activity to record work at this stage.

 Area of study 2

LOOKING AT THE VARIETY OF LIFE

 C2

Purpose
To introduce children to the wide variety of life to be found in their own immediate environment.

Materials needed
Viewing jars, perspex tank with lid, animal cages and equipment, potted plants (or a garden).

Activity 1: Walk around the school
Take a walk around the school, inside and out, looking at all the plants and animals you can find – from potted plants, grassed lawns and moss on window frames to school pets, stray dogs, wild birds and the mini-beasts which abound in every nook and cranny. Encourage the children to use all their senses to describe their experience and feelings. You can use questions such as: What does the moss feel like? Can you smell anything under this stone? What do you see on this spider's web?

If you bring any mini-beasts into the classroom for a short period, put them in viewing jars or a perspex tank with some soil or turf and a secure lid. Ensure that you observe DES regulations about animals in school and do make sure the children are involved in some part of their care to reinforce the idea that they are living. You should return them to their habitat as soon as possible.

vivarium

Activity 2: Look at school pets
If you have or can bring in to school any small, safe pets, discuss the similarities and differences of size, shape, body covering, colour, teeth, movement and general behaviour.

Activity 3: Look at plants
The school and its immediate environment should, with luck, contain a large collection of different types of plants. These may range from indoor pot plants, cultivated areas of garden and lawn to trees, agricultural land, and wild overgrown corners and unusual places. Discuss similarities and differences between plants you find, looking at their site, size, colour, fruits, root formation, etc. If possible visit a local nursery or farm.

Activity 4: Look at large animals
Try to visit a zoo, safari park or farm and observe the animals in their living quarters. You may be able to show the children video material of the wild animals in their natural environment, which would be a useful comparison, even at this age. On the visit, encourage the children to use all their senses to try and remember their observations for discussion later in school.

Recording work
All of these activities will provide material for assembly, stimulation for writing (when possible), painting, modelling, drawing, music and movement and role-play in the home corner. You could turn the home corner into a vet's surgery, a zoo, a garden centre or a pet shop.

Take a tape recorder with you on your trips and record not only the sounds the animals make but also the children's comments. You could make a quiz of the animal sounds when you get back to school.

For further ideas see *Blueprints: Topics* on pets and *Blueprints: Assemblies* for assemblies on colour, signs and signals and the seasons.

Copymasters
Use copymaster 2 (Our walk) for the children to record observations using all the senses. On return to school and after your discussion on the trip, the children can record their observations on this sheet by drawing one picture to represent something they remember observing with each of their senses. They can also underwrite the beginning of the observation, 'I saw . . .', etc.

Discourage the children from tasting anything they find growing wild or elsewhere. You can make the point by drawing a red cross in the 'I tasted' box. However, if you visit somewhere such as a dairy where it might be legitimate to taste then the box can be used.

 VARIETY OF PEOPLE

Area of study 3

Purpose
To show the great variety of human life.

Materials needed
Photographs and cuttings from magazines of many different racial types; photographs of the children and their families; pictures of people of different ages: babies, children, teenagers, adults, old people.

Activity
Make a display of the photographs collected and discuss the similarities and differences between the various ethnic groups. Talk (sensitively) about skin colour, eyes, lips, noses and hair and try to find the similarities between the races. Obviously you will want to stress the fact that we are all human and have equal rights, despite the physical differences and differences of custom and behaviour.

Look at the photographs of the different age groups and discuss growing up and growing older. List the differences between babies and grown-ups and grand-parents. Ask the children to put the photographs in the correct order for age and size of person.

Try to arrange for a family to visit school so that children can compare body sizes and family similarities of skin, hair and eye colour and other features. Any discussions of families will need tactful handling for those children who are adopted or who come from a one-parent family.

Copymasters

Use copymaster 3 (People) for gathering information and focusing attention on similarities and differences between children and between people generally.

You can use the pictures as elements of a graph by cutting out the pictures you need to show distribution of hair, eye and skin colour in the class.

The family picture can also be used for a graph to show family size.

child's own picture of family

4 people

3 people

5 people

How many in your family?

Attainment target 3: Processes of life

Pupils should develop their knowledge and understanding of the organisation of living things and of the processes which characterise their survival and reproduction.

Level 1

Statements of attainment

Pupils should:

- be able to name or label the external parts of the human body/plants, for example, *arm, leg/flower, stem.*

Area of study 1: IDENTIFYING PARTS OF THE HUMAN BODY   C4

Purpose
To identify parts of the human body through observation, discussion and play.

Materials needed
A collection of dolls, action men and other articulated figures, a home corner, hospital dressing-up clothes, assorted cardboard boxes for dolls' beds, small bandages, paints, crayons, paper, scissors, sticky-backed Velcro®.

Activity 1: Poems and rhymes
Using finger rhymes, nursery rhymes, poems and songs, introduce the idea of parts of the body being universal. Songs and rhymes can include 'Heads and shoulders, knees and toes', 'The hokey cokey', 'Here we go round the mulberry bush'. Two lesser known ones which are fun are:

'I wiggle my fingers, I wiggle my toes
I wiggle my shoulders, I wiggle my nose,
There are no more wiggles left in me,
Now I'm as still as still as can be.'

'Clap clap hands, one two three,
Put your hands upon your knee,
Lift them high to touch the sky,
Clap, clap hands and away they fly.'

Activity 2: 'Simon says'
Gather the children together and play a game such as 'Simon says'. 'Simon' gives directions for moving parts of the body, sometimes in amusing ways, e.g. 'Simon says touch your shoulder with your tongue'. The important thing of course is that children are only to follow the instruction if it is prefaced by the words, 'Simon says', otherwise they are out. Picture flash cards can be used instead of words for identifying different parts of the body, and if you write the word on the reverse of the card and use this sometimes, it will help build up sight vocabulary.

reverse

Activity 3: Make a picture/reading game
These flash cards can be used in conjunction with a large picture of the human body, the cards acting as labels for the various body parts. Put sticky-backed Velcro® on the back of the cards so that you can re-use

4

them as part of a guessing/reading game. For example a small group of children can hold up two cards and ask the others to guess which one says or is a picture of a leg. If they get the right answer they can put the word on the large picture themselves, if wrong then you can point to the limb and then the child can put on the word. The game can be played using the picture or the word.

Activity 4: Create a dolls' hospital
Using for stimulus a real life story of an accident involving a broken limb or a story of a broken doll, turn your home corner into a dolls' hospital. Make suitable posters and larger labels, saying for example, 'Casualty', 'Way in' and use an assortment of different sized cardboard boxes as beds for the school dolls or those which the children bring in. You will also need simple bedding and one or two doctor and nurse outfits and several short crêpe or gauze bandages. Try to obtain X-ray photographs of different parts of the body which

you can use as part of your discussion and then stick to the window as part of your display on the body. Part of your discussion can be about safety and the limbs or parts of the body which are most easily damaged or broken.

Activity 5: Paint a self-portrait
The children can paint or draw self-portraits or portraits of their friends. When the picture is finished discuss whether each part of the body is in the correct place, and whether all the parts are present. If not, the child can add to or alter the picture accordingly.

Activity 6: Copymasters
Use copymaster 4 (Rainbow body) to help the children identify and name the different parts of the body and also reinforce the concept of colour.

 Area of study 2 | # USING THE BODY C5 ▶

Purpose
To show that we use different parts of the body for different activities and to encourage more body awareness and an understanding of the capabilities and limitations of different parts of the body.

Materials needed
Photographs and videos of sporting events, games and pastimes (for both able-bodied and disabled people), pencils, crayons, paper and small PE apparatus.

Activity 1: Use PE
Using a PE lesson, ask the children to do things which emphasise use of different parts of the body. These can include:

- Using the legs when running, walking, skipping, jumping
- Moving around the hall without using legs

- Throwing and retrieving such small apparatus as balls and bags
- Carrying small apparatus without use of hands
- Pushing small apparatus without using hands or feet.

Activity 2: Use music
Use music and movement lesson times further to develop body awareness by asking the children to make different shapes with their bodies, e.g. spiky, rounded, tall and thin, short and squat. Use suitable music to create the mood.

Activity 3: Watch videos
Watch video extracts of hobbies and pastimes and discuss with the children which parts of the body are

We use these parts of our body for our hobby.

hands — whole body — eyes — ears — legs — head

different colour for each set

magazine cut-outs of hobbies and sports

used in pursuit of such activities as piano playing, javelin throwing, swimming, running, horse riding, fishing, archery and so on. Try to find extracts of disabled sports people and discuss how they may have overcome their particular difficulties.

Activity 4: Sorting and classifying

Sort your collection of pictures into sets of activities which use different parts of the body. Stick them on to paper and display them as sets (see illustration on page 5).

Subsets may be too complex at this stage so simply repeat any pictures using several parts of the body in as many sets as necessary, e.g. in piano playing the head, arms, hands and body are used.

Copymasters

Use copymaster 5 (Things I do with my body) to record the activities described. After discussion, children are to circle the parts of the body used for each activity and then colour in the picture depicting that activity.

PLANTS

C6

Purpose

To observe similarities and differences between plants and to identify their different parts.

Materials needed

Gardening catalogues, scissors, glue, pot plants, garden area, jam jars, water, old tights, eggshells, grass and cress seed, broad bean seeds, pencils, paper, crayons.

Activity 1: Plant spotting

Go for a plant-spotting walk around school. Look for cultivated and wild plants and look for any unusual places where plants grow. Try to find small plants such as mosses, fungi and algae as well as observing larger ones such as trees. After explaining what weeds are, pull one up to examine the root system. For recording work, children can draw or paint from direct observations.

Do identify and avoid poisonous plants such as fungi, and trees such as laburnums which have poisonous seeds. Also point out dandelions which are difficult to uproot because of their long tap roots and which leave a very pungent odour on the hands.

Activity 2: Go on a visit

Visit an overgrown inner city plot, woodland, farmland, or a well maintained park with cultivated flower beds. Use a tape recorder or a camera to record impressions and the variety of plants.

Activity 3: Take cuttings

Take cuttings of quick rooters such as tradescantia, spider plant and geranium and watch root growth start in a jar of water. Note the day you took the cutting and count the number of days until root growth starts.

Activity 4: Grow seeds

Grow cress in eggshell 'heads'. Note the shape of the leaves and break open one egg head (yours!) to observe the root system.

Grow grass seed in the toes of old tights to make 'punk' heads.

Grass-head punks

toe of tights
knot
seeds pushed in
compost
water

grass shoots

features painted
in waterproof pen

saucer

Grow flower seeds if you have a patch of school garden or a window-box. The most successful outdoor germinaters are nasturtium, Virginia stock, candytuft, nigella, or calendula. Grow broad bean seeds to compare germination of a larger seed. You do not need to use the word 'germination' at this level. Grow the beans in jam jars with a cotton wool wick to observe the roots and plant some in compost to find out which group grow better. Try to get the children to notice the difference.

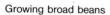
Growing broad beans

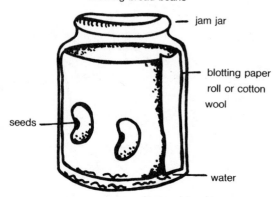

jam jar

blotting paper roll or cotton wool

seeds

water

Activity 5: Sorting and classifying
Look through gardening catalogues and get the children to cut out pictures of different plants they like and then sort them for colour and shape of flower and leaf.

Copymasters
Use copymaster 6 (Plants) to reinforce the names of the parts of a plant and to give practice in completion of a picture.

Attainment target 4: Genetics and evolution

Pupils should develop their knowledge and understanding of variation and its genetic and environmental causes and the basic mechanisms of inheritance, selection and evolution.

Statements of attainment

Pupils should:

● know that human beings vary from one individual to the next.

 DIFFERENCES IN PEOPLE

Area of study 1 · C7

Purpose
To show that there are differences of age, sex, size and colour between people.

Materials needed
Paper, felt pens/crayons, two colours of activity paper, photographs of children's families, crêpe paper or large PE hoops as markers for sets.

Activity 1
Gather the children together for a class or group discussion of visible differences between them. Using the children as examples try to bring out the following:

a) The physical differences between boys and girls (at your discretion) and the numbers of boys and girls in the class.

Using a crêpe paper strip or a large PE hoop stapled to the wall, make two sets circles, one for each sex. Using name tabs backed with Blu-Tack® get each child to put their name in the correct set. You can use self-portraits as an alternative (see below).

b) The different racial groups represented in the class, as shown by skin colour.

Make as many set rings as there are colours of skin and using the self-portraits from the last exercise, re-group according to skin colour. If there is only one racial type represented in class make an empty set to show this but find posters of people with different coloured skins, to illustrate the point.

c) The different sizes of children in your class.

As part of your discussion and getting the children themselves to help make the assessment of relative size, group the class in order of height. This will be the most tactful aspect of size to record. Make a bar graph of the relative heights. Comparing size will be an important part of your maths teaching at this stage.

d) The ages of children in the class.

You may already have a class birthday chart which you can use to help you talk about the time when each child's age alters. Using this as a starting point, divide the children into the appropriate age groups and record the findings on a pair of clowns, as shown overleaf.

'Age' clowns

Move the child's name balloon to the appropriate clown, when necessary, during the year.

Copymasters
Use copymaster 7 (Are you a boy or girl?) either as a personal record of the child's sex, or as blanks for any of the sets exercises mentioned above. The child fills in his or her own name on the correct picture and colours it in. The opposite picture then serves as a comparison.

 FACES

Purpose
To show that our faces are the first indicators of age, sex, race, as well as of emotion and individuality.

Materials needed
Paper, pencils, crayons, photographs of the children's families, several hand mirrors, posters of people of many racial origins and age, paper plates, activity paper.

Activity 1
Discuss the shape of human faces generally and draw one yourself, pointing out the positioning of features.

Get the children to do self-portraits (they can use the hand mirrors to remind themselves of important features such as eye and hair colour) and then portraits of friends, either in crayon or paint. A useful follow up discussion would include consideration of what makes faces individual: features such as skin colour, hair colour and style and eye colour. Have a guessing game using the finished portraits, to see if the children can identify characteristic features of classmates. Talk about features which the children think make their friends' faces look nice.

Activity 2
Talk about features which differ according to racial origin, such as face, eye, nose and mouth shape, colour of skin and colour and texture of hair. Use posters or the children themselves to illustrate the features.

Activity 3
Talk about the changes which age makes to faces. Use the children's family photographs to illustrate similarity of family features and the changes of age.

Activity 4
Discuss emotions which the children feel and the times when they feel them, as well as the changes these feelings produce on their faces and bodies.

Make double-sided puppets with paper plates and use them in drama activities such as story telling or in your discussions about emotions.

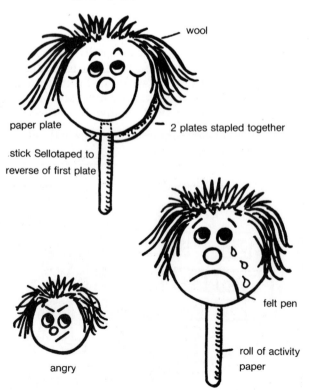

Speaking faces

wool

paper plate

2 plates stapled together

stick Sellotaped to reverse of first plate

felt pen

roll of activity paper

angry

Copymasters

Use copymaster 8 (Faces) to consolidate discussion of faces. The child is to add his or her own hairstyle, eye colour, mouth, nose and skin colour to the large outline of a face. He or she is then to choose among the faces in the boxes the one which is most like his or her own with regard to age and sex.

 ## VARIETY OF SKILLS

Purpose

To show that people have different skills and can do some things better than others.

Materials needed

Paints, crayons, paper, small PE apparatus.

Activity 1

During one PE lesson ask the children to see how many different activities they can do. Ask them to walk, run, hop, skip, roll, balance, throw and catch. It need only be competitive in the sense of the child competing against himself/herself. The children can decide which skills they are good at, and which they are still learning to master. It is advisable to be very positive in an exercise of this nature.

Activity 2

Over a few days, enable each child to participate in a wide range of classroom activities. Point out to them which of the following skills they are good at: reading, writing, drawing, painting, crafts, constructional activities, music, drama and so on.

To consolidate the activity have a class discussion on your findings. Try to instil in the children the fact that everyone is good at something and through group discussion draw from them which skills each person in the class has. It is essential that this discussion brings out at least one skill for each child.

Copymasters

Use copymaster 9 (Things I am good at) to record this activity. The child looks at the picture and decides which of the activities he or she is good at. He or she can then circle or colour in the appropriate pictures. Part of the value of recording activities of this kind is the conversation which goes on in the process between peers and with adults.

Attainment target 5: Human influences on the Earth

Pupils should develop knowledge and understanding of the ways in which human activities affect the Earth.

 ### Statements of attainment

Pupils should:

● know that human activities produce a wide range of waste products.

 ## WHICH ARE WASTE PRODUCTS?

Purpose

To identify the waste products that the children will commonly see.

Materials needed

Plastic gloves and bags, tweezers.

Activity

Take a walk around school as a class or in small groups and try to find examples of waste. The sorts of area where you might look could include the school kitchen, litter bins, the class waste bin, garden areas and toilets. Here you can talk about our bodies taking the good things out of the food we eat and leaving the rest. The solid matter produced is the waste matter of our bodies. Visit the school boiler room with the caretaker and if the central heating is fired by solid fuel try to find any waste products, such as ashes. Talk about the smoke and soot produced.

Take a camera and/or a tape recorder with you as

you search the school in order to record instant impressions. If a clean-up is needed in any area, the photos will serve to record the need. Collect any of the cleaner waste products to make a display for the classroom, e.g. a few grass clippings with a magazine photo of a lawn or lawn mower; a piece of broken brick, next to a photo of a house being built and so on.

Copymasters
Use copymaster 10 (Mr Litter) to record, in a construc-

tive way, the waste products you found. The children can colour in the parts of Mr Litter's body which they found on the walk, whether in the correct place (i.e. litter bin) or not. The exercise is concerned with identifying wastes.

strong white card

drawing or painting of person

We have been busy!

glue

magazine cut-out

activity paper

This is what is left when you mow the lawn.

PRODUCING WASTE

Area of study 2 — C11

Purpose
To identify those activities which produce waste products.

Materials needed
A bowl of warm water for hand washing, soap, cloth towel, paper towels.

Activity 1
Select the 10 children with the dirtiest pairs of hands after playtime. After discussing the state of these hands, get five to wash their hands in the bowl and dry them with paper towels. Get the remainder to wash and then dry their hands on the cloth towel. You can then discuss where the dirt from the hands has gone and what will happen to the three waste products: the water, the paper and the dirt on the cloth.

Activity 2
Discuss what the children do during the day that produces waste of different sorts. For example:

Activity	Waste products
Washing	Dirty water
Going to the toilet	Toilet paper and water
Breakfast	Cereal packets, bottles, crusts, washing-up water

Journey to school	Exhaust fumes from vehicles
School work	Paper, pencil shavings, paint
Break	Sweet and crisp wrappings, fruit skins
Lunch	Left over food, washing-up water
Break	Sweet and crisp wrappers, fruit skins
Journey home	Exhaust fumes
Playing at home	Broken toys, dust, mud on floor
Evening meal	Waste food, packets

Copymasters
Use copymaster 11 (Where did it come from?) to record this activity. The child is to match the activities shown with the appropriate waste product.

WASTE IN THE ENVIRONMENT

C12

Purpose
To show how waste affects the environment.

Materials needed
A selection of slides and videos on general pollution of air, water and land (choose short, dramatic shots in both media to compare these with areas of beauty and litter free areas), camera, tape recorder, collection of different packages and containers, posters of polluted areas and beauty spots.

Activity 1
Show the slides or videos and look at the posters and discuss the causes and effects of waste and pollution. With the help of your other visual aids, contrast the polluted areas with those that are litter free or which are areas of natural beauty. You can ask the children which they think is best.

Activity 2
Take a walk around school and/or the local area. Look for areas which are polluted with litter and rubbish. If possible photograph these for inclusion in a class display. Record the children's reactions on tape.

Activity 3
Use the different empty packages and containers for 'junk modelling'.

You could even try to think of ways to recycle packages into useful items, e.g. make a pencil container from a cocoa tin.

Copymasters
Use copymaster 12 (Where is it?) to record this activity. On the large picture of the street, children have to pick out the items which are waste products and circle them.

Attainment target 6: Types and uses of materials

Pupils should develop their knowledge and understanding of the properties of materials and the way properties of materials determine their uses and form the basis for their classification.

Level 1

Statements of attainment

Pupils should:

● be able to describe familiar and unfamiliar objects in terms of simple properties, for example, *shape, colour, texture*, and describe how they behave when they are, for example, *squashed and stretched*.

LOOKING AT SHAPE

C13

Purpose
To recognise the different plane and solid shapes in everyday objects and to describe how they behave.

Materials needed
A bag of everyday groceries including tins, packets, bottles, bags and some fruits and vegetables; a range of common everyday objects such as oval place mats, a rectangular tray, a circular plate, a square tablecloth, a spherical teapot, a cylindrical mug; pictures of the larger household items such as a cube-shaped tumble drier and a cuboid-shaped washing machine, fridge and wardrobe; dolls' house furniture, a collection of 3D wooden shapes, illustrations of plane shapes, Plasticine® and balloons.

Activity 1: Plane shapes
You will already have planned activities about shape (2D and 3D) as part of your maths programme. (See also a topic on this subject in *Blueprints: Topics* in this series.)

Once the children are beginning to be familiar with the 2D shapes have a game of 'I spy shapes in the classroom', with clues such as 'It has three sides and three corners' or more simply 'I spy a square'.

Activity 2
Make a 'shape clown' from coloured and textured paper, to act as an illustration and vocabulary sheet (see overleaf).

Shape clown

Cellophane cut-outs

Mr. Shape

Blu-Tack®

activity paper

crepe paper frill

shape decorations
in sticky paper

Activity 3
Play a matching game with the shape clown. Make cards the same size and colour as the shapes on the picture and ask the children to match them with the picture. The word can go on the reverse and can be used as reading competence grows.

Activity 4
Use art and craft time to reinforce shape. Cut out the common shapes you are using in many different colours and sizes and allow the children to experiment with making pictures, patterns and tessellations.

Activity 5: Solid shapes
In the initial stages of identification of solid shape, look for the common shapes in toys, classroom items and groceries. Bring in a bag of groceries (as listed on page 11) and sort the various packets and jars into sets of different shapes.

Activity 6
Use dolls' house furniture to sort for shape. Make a display of 3D wooden shapes and this furniture to illustrate the link. Use photos of common household items as part of the display.

Activity 7
Look at the properties of solid shapes for building and movement. See if they will roll, slide, tessellate. See what the children can build with cylinders, cuboids, cubes, spheres and triangular prisms. The cost of such shapes bought as sets from manufacturers is usually astronomical, so try to find a parent who will make a good number from wood. Balls can be used as spheres.

Activity 8
Using Plasticine® or clay get the children to attempt to make the shapes. Show them how to make spheres, cylinders, cubes, bowl shapes (thumb pots) and any other odd shapes by simply squeezing the clay in their fist. Then ask them to see how these shapes move down a steep slope. Change the shapes by squeezing, flattening, stretching and rolling. See if they behave in the same way.

Activity 9
Play with balloons, sponges, cotton wool, washing-up bottles and soft drinks cans. Use the balloons deflated and inflated and test them and the other shapes and materials for bounce, squashability, spring and release. By observing shape and material you will be paving the

way for work on textures. Discuss whether the objects/containers you have are a suitable shape for their purpose and whether changing their shape alters this.

Use the children's construction models (which can be photographed) and their art work and conversation to record this work.

Copymasters

Use copymaster 13 (Look at shapes) for a completion exercise to record this activity. The child is to complete the picture by adding the missing limbs to the shape man.

Purpose
To recognise different colours and to experiment with changing them.

Materials needed
Paint, coloured ink, paper, fabric, coloured Cellophane, tissue paper, a collection of everyday objects in the primary colours (red, blue, yellow, black and white) and also pink, purple, brown, green.

Activity 1
Make a colour corner each week from the start of term, as part of your usual teaching for colour recognition. Include the children's own toys and household items in these displays.

Activity 2
When painting, show the children how to mix the primary colours to produce orange, green and purple and how to lighten and darken colours using black and white. Encourage them to add a little at a time of any second colour so that the gradual change can be observed. The changes involved in this type of activity will be the source of much discussion and the children will need to have plenty of time to practise techniques and to experiment for themselves.

Activity 3
Bring in a shopping bag full of fruit and vegetables which can form the subject of a useful colour sorting activity. Sharing out some of the fruit to be eaten may serve to fix the learning experience.

Activity 4
Make a simple Lotto game with colour as the only feature, using the brightly coloured sticky paper and covering the boards with sticky-backed plastic (such as Contact® or Fablon®). Children can play with an adult or an older child in groups of two to four.

Activity 5
As an extension of colour and an introduction to light as a topic, introduce the word 'transparent'. Look through different coloured Cellophane and observe the apparent changes to normal colours. Overlap the Cellophane to get colour mixes. Try to find some

examples of stained glass windows and let the children see how the coloured glass casts a coloured light.

Make stained glass windows in the classroom, using black activity paper as the frame. Glue coloured tissue or Cellophane to the reverse.

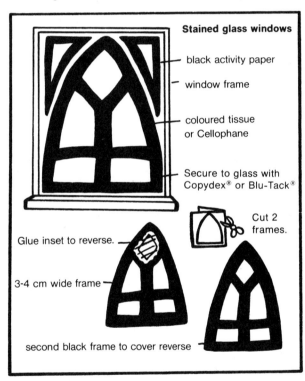

Stained glass windows
- black activity paper
- window frame
- coloured tissue or Cellophane
- Secure to glass with Copydex® or Blu-Tack®

Glue inset to reverse.
3-4 cm wide frame
Cut 2 frames.
second black frame to cover reverse

Make sunglasses from a frame of coloured card and an inset of coloured Cellophane, or sun visors using the same method.

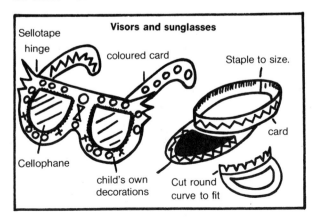

Visors and sunglasses
Sellotape hinge
coloured card
Staple to size.
card
Cellophane
child's own decorations
Cut round curve to fit

Activity 6

As a contrast, introduce the word 'opaque' by painting pictures on the windows. The opaque colour blocks out the light and creates shade to a varying degree, depending on the thickness of the paint.

Copymasters

Use copymaster 14 (Fruit colours) for the children to record their work on this activity. The child has to colour the fruits (and objects) in the correct colour.

 Area of study 3

LOOKING AT TEXTURE

 C15

Purpose

To identify different textures.

Materials needed

A collection of everyday objects made of different materials as in Area of Study 1. Have examples of wood, metal, fabrics, plastic, glass, stone, concrete, rubber and as many contrasting textures as possible to illustrate vocabulary such as rough, smooth, slippery, squelchy, sticky, tacky, springy, soft, hard, bumpy, abrasive, crackly, brittle, knobbly, spongy. 'Scarecrow' visual aid of different textures and a 'Feely' box.

Activity 1

Have an initial discussion about texture using the children's clothes and objects in the classroom as examples.

Activity 2

Make a visual aid in the form of a collage of a scarecrow made from a variety of different materials, e.g. wood shavings, fabrics, metal and plastic buttons, leather and so on. Display this at a convenient height for the children to touch. You can also display a few examples of vocabulary on the appropriate materials.

Activity 3

Make a 'Feely' box from a cardboard box with a closable lid. You will need to cut a hand-sized hole at either side so that a child can put in both hands to feel the mystery object. The idea is that the teacher or another child puts about six small objects into the box, unseen by the 'player', who then has to guess the contents by feeling. Change the contents for each player and include such objects as small toy cars, stones, pine cones, an apple or a piece of plastic.

Activity 4

Play 'Blind man's buff' in which the children have to guess the identity of players they catch by feeling them.

Recording work

As part of your art and craft provision the children can make collages of anything which interests them. Provide a range of ready cut fabric scraps of different sizes, bits of wood, old screws, wire, wool, cork, polystyrene chips and other objects with interesting textures.

Copymasters

Use copymaster 15 (Materials I found) to record this activity. The child has to sort through a collection of ready cut scraps of materials (each about 2 cm square) and match them to the descriptions shown.

Attainment target 9: Earth and atmosphere

Pupils should develop their knowledge and understanding of the structure and main features of the Earth, the atmosphere and their changes over time.

Level 1

Statements of attainment

Pupils should:

- know that there is a variety of weather conditions.
- be able to describe changes in the weather.

Area of study 1

DIFFERENT KINDS OF WEATHER

C16

Purpose
To identify different weather conditions.

Materials needed
A selection of different types of clothes such as swimming costumes, raincoats, scarves, umbrellas, wellingtons, ear muffs, sun hats; photographs of many different types of weather conditions such as snow, rain, hail, fog, mist, wind, sunshine; videos of weather conditions or weather forecasts, a collection of stories and poems about the weather.

Activity 1
Read poems and stories and discuss the children's experiences of different types of weather. Some may not have had any experience of snow whereas others may have been on a skiing holiday or to a very hot country. Discuss the children's favourite weather.

Activity 2
Dress several children in the different kinds of clothes and discuss in what sort of weather the children might wear such clothes. Relate this to the pictures of weather you have collected. Sunday magazines are good sources of such pictures.

Activity 3
Using video material, stories and poems as stimulus, the children can draw, paint or write about their own reminiscences of an event or trip which took place in one of the types of weather.

Activity 4
Turn the home corner into a clothes shop with a seasonal flavour. As part of your work on time you may want to discuss the seasons and the different types of weather associated with them. The clothes shop could sell summer clothes for a few days, winter clothes for the next few and so on. Decorate the shop with holiday posters and weather pictures. You may want to make a point about the difference between climate and weather by pointing out that some parts of the world have mostly summer type weather and so on.

Copymasters
Use copymaster 16 (What shall I wear?). The illustration shows three children, one in a swimsuit, one in a raincoat, one in winter clothes. The children have to draw in the appropriate type of weather around the child, referring to the weather symbols at the bottom of the picture.

Area of study 2

CHANGES IN THE WEATHER

C17

Purpose
To observe and recognise changes in the weather.

Materials needed
A weather house, wind vane, pine cone, barometer, thermometer and any other indicators of weather change that are available, video of a weather forecast, collection of poems and stories on weather folklore, photographs and pictures of different things being affected by the weather, e.g. trees blown down in gales, cars buried under the snow, reservoirs dried up in a drought.

Activity 1
Record the daily weather forecast on video or on audio tape and discuss the changes from the day before. Later you can discuss if the forecast was correct.

Activity 2
Observe the weather throughout the day and look at the sky. Try to recognise indicators of weather change such as different types of cloud, the colour of the sky, the wind freshening, movement on the surface of ponds, rivers or puddles, the Sun disappearing behind clouds, rain, mist and fog.

Activity 3

Look at the different indicators of change and discuss what to look for when recognising the different weather conditions. Observe a wind vane, weather house or pine cones for a few days to see if and when they show some change. Use a thermometer to show change in temperature. Put it in full sunlight and then in a cool, shady place. At this stage merely show the children the registration of change by the level of the mercury in the tube. Ensure that they understand that the higher up the tube it is, the hotter the weather is.

Activity 4

Read the weather poems and folklore and discuss whether there is any truth in them.

Copymasters

Use copymaster 17 (A day out) to record work on this activity. The sheet shows a series of pictures of a picnic being spoiled by sudden bad weather. The pictures are not in the correct sequence. The children have to cut up the sheet, rearrange the pictures and glue them on to a second sheet in the correct order. Look at the sheets with the children. Discuss the different signs of weather change in each picture to help them rearrange the pictures in the correct order.

RECORDING CHANGES IN THE WEATHER

Area of study 3   C18

Purpose

To introduce the children to simple recording of weather.

Materials needed

A daily weather change chart (see illustration below).

A weather change calendar:

Activity 1

As part of your class routine use a weather change and daily calendar such as the Ladybird one shown. Take a minute each day to note the day, date and weather with the class. Children can take it in turns to change the chart.

Activity 2

Observe and discuss the changes in the weather during each school day for one week. Use the simple chart shown to record changes during the day.

Copymasters

Use copymaster 18 (Weather record) for the children to record these observations. Set aside 10 minutes at the end of the afternoon for the children to draw the symbols for the weather that day in the boxes at the side of each day. They can then add the Sun or Moon in the sky as appropriate.

Attainment target 10: Forces

Pupils should develop their knowledge and understanding of forces; their nature, significance and effects on the movement of objects.

Level
1

Statements of attainment

Pupils should:

● know that things can be moved by pushing them.

Area of study 1

BODY POWER

Purpose
To show that things can be moved by pushing with different parts of the body.

Materials needed
Small toys and assorted materials: toy cars and other vehicles, balls of assorted sizes (from ping-pong ball to football), blocks of wood, large rockery stones, small plastic counters, balloons, toy boats, paper gliders, paper, glue, pens.

Large toys: scooter, rocking horse, bicycle, skate-board, roller boots, toy pram or pushchair, toddler's brick trolley, full size pushchair.

Small PE apparatus: bean bags, balls, quoits; use of local park or children's play area; sand-pit or sand tray, small earth-moving toys and sand play tools.

Pictures of things which are pushed or which push (e.g. prams, trolleys, trains shunting, bikes, scooters, the wind blowing trees or washing, yachts, clouds, smoke in the air, water weeds in a river).

Activity 1
Most of these activities are best done in small groups so that the children can get maximum hands-on experience for themselves and maximum involvement in conversation. You will need an adult present to guide the talk and the activity.

Even young children have experience of pushing heavy things and they can quickly understand that moving heavy things from a standstill (overcoming the inertia) needs a transfer of energy from them to the object in order to create the movement. It is not so easy to detect this in very light objects.

Discuss the idea of pushing heavy things and what things they have to push themselves, e.g. pushing a door open, pushing a friend on a swing, pushing a button to start something or pushing a full super-market trolley.

There are many toys on the market that rely on pushing and the children will enjoy bringing them in to show the class.

Set out the small toys and assorted materials on a level uncarpeted area of floor. Allow the children the opportunity to play and experiment with pushing the various things. To focus attention on the parts of the body that are doing the pushing, ask questions such

as: What part of your body did you use to start off the push? What happens if you push gently or you push hard? Which part of your body pushed the hardest? Do you always have to push forwards to make a thing move forwards? Which things could you push the farthest? Which things went forwards on their own after you started them off?

Activity 2
Look at the pictures and discuss what is being pushed or what is pushing something else. Make two sets of things which you may want to display. If you have time for a walk around the neighbourhood or even around school you may be able to spot some of these things.

Activity 3
Play in the sand tray. Alter the texture by adding water and pebbles. Encourage the children to make tunnels, hills, holes, slopes and flat surfaces using the sand play tools, the toy vehicles and their hands to push the sand around.

Activity 4
Experiment with the large toys, letting the children take turns on everything. Ask questions such as the ones suggested in Activity 1 above. Other questions might include: Do you need to ride the toy to make it move forwards? Was it hard work to get the object to move at first? How many parts of your body did you use to push? What happens if you push someone on a toy? Which is the heaviest thing you can push?

Be careful not to overload small vehicles with too many children. Make basic safety rules such as:

● Do not lift any object which you find too heavy.
● Do not push vehicles into walls, especially when carrying friends.
● Watch where you are going when riding a toy vehicle and do not go too fast.

Whilst observing all necessary safety rules you may like to try pushing something very heavy on wheels such as the school piano. It may take quite a bit of co-operative behaviour and movement energy to get it going and some care to stop it.

Activity 3

Use the small PE apparatus to experiment with long distance pushing of objects such as balls, quoits and bean bags. Set up a little test to see which object could be pushed the farthest. At this stage allow each child to have a turn at pushing each object with their hands. Introduce the variables of throwing, rolling and kicking, and discuss what the children observe. Do not get involved in details of added momentum yet.

Activity 4

Visit a local park or children's play area and investigate the effect of pushing on the large apparatus there.

Additional factors are involved here such as the effect of gravity on objects pushed down the slide, the working of a pendulum as on the swings and the circular movement of the roundabout. At this stage concentrate the children's attention on the part of their body used to start the push and keep it going.

Copymasters

Use copymaster 19 (How did you push these things?) to record experience of this activity. It is a simple sorting and classifying activity involving the children in matching parts of their body used to push the object they moved.

Area of study 2

AIR POWER

C20

Purpose

To show that air can push things.

Materials needed

Sand tray, water tray, toy yacht, wheel, wooden bricks, small toys, footballs, ping-pong balls, balloons, washing-up liquid bottles, margarine tubs, straws, feathers, small rocks, paper, card, glue, drawing ink or thin paint mix.

Activity 1

The children will be using their body energy to create the wind which will in turn move the objects. Try to get them to see that this is different in origin from the atmospheric wind which also moves things.

Activity 2

Using the collection of small toys and junk items allow the children to experiment freely with them to see how many they can get to move by blowing on them. (Point out that they are then pushing the objects with air.) Make two sets from the objects: those which can be moved by blowing and those which cannot.

Activity 2

'Blob and blow' is an art technique which illustrates how air can push things. Put blobs of drawing ink or

watery paint on to paper and using a drinking straw to direct the runs of liquid blow the blobs into fantastic shapes.

Activity 3

Have a tub race, using plastic margarine tubs and a shiny hall floor or smooth table top. Invert the tubs and allow each child to blow his or her own along a given course. The blowers will need to blow on to the side of the tub. Try using balloons as the source of air power. Blow one up. Hold the opening and direct the escaping air on to the tub. An empty washing-up liquid bottle can also be used to puff the tub along.

Activity 4

Using the water tray, get the children to select some of the small items which float and let them experiment with manual pushing (to link with Activity 1) and blowing. You can ask questions such as: Which things can you move by blowing? Do they move along in a fairly straight line or do they bob around on the spot? Which thing moved the fastest and which the slowest?

Activity 5

Make a yacht from a margarine tub, a straw and paper as shown below.

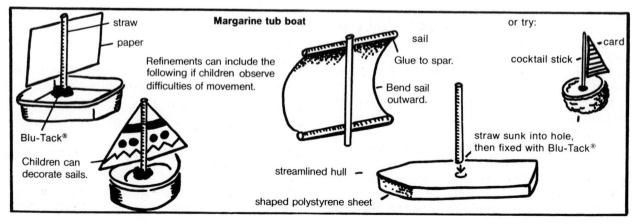

Try different shaped sails and try blowing the boats from different directions. See what happens. Does the boat move sideways, forwards, or round and round?

Copymasters
Use copymaster 20 (The mighty wind race) to consolidate work on this activity. It is a game for two players involving counting up to three. There are 10 places on the track. Instead of a dice you will need a toy windmill with its sails marked 1, 2, 3, 0, 1, 2, 3, 0, if it has eight wings and folds. Toy windmills can be bought cheaply or you can make your own, as shown below.

Using this as a dice substitute will help reinforce the idea of air as a power and will also be great fun. The child blows the windmill and when it stops, the number on the wing which lies nearest the stick is the number of places the child can move.

Cut out little card yachts and fix them with Blu-Tack® to a plastic counter for use as counters in the game.

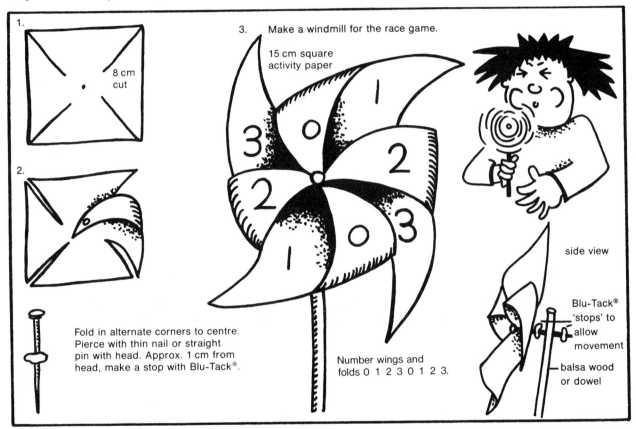

1.
8 cm cut

2.

Fold in alternate corners to centre. Pierce with thin nail or straight pin with head. Approx. 1 cm from head, make a stop with Blu-Tack®.

3. Make a windmill for the race game.

15 cm square activity paper

Number wings and folds 0 1 2 3 0 1 2 3.

side view

Blu-Tack® 'stops' to allow movement

balsa wood or dowel

 Area of study 3 | **WATER POWER** | C21

Purpose
To show that water can move things.

Materials needed
All the items from 'Air power' (see opposite) plus the following: hose pipe, water tap, bucket, washing-up liquid bottles, water play toys, toy water wheel, watering cans, foil pie plate, an old pencil.

Activity 1
Hold the margarine tub race using the washing-up liquid bottles full of water as the propellant. Outdoors is probably the best venue!

Activity 2
Let the children take it in turns to move footballs and ping-pong balls using the hose pipe. See who can push the different balls the farthest. Pose questions

such as: What happens if the water squirts quickly? What happens if the water squirts slowly? Can you make the balls move where you want them to go?

Activity 3
Using the water tray, toy water wheel and the watering can or a tap, experiment with the wheel to see how the water pushes the wheel around. Ask them if they can make the wheel turn first quickly and then slowly.

A simple water wheel can be made from a foil pie plate as shown overleaf. Hold it under a running tap.

Activity 4
Using an assortment of heavy/light and large/small objects let the children experiment with pushing them with water. The objects can be propelled by jets of water from the washing-up liquid bottles or by waves of water from a small bucket sluiced along the ground.

19

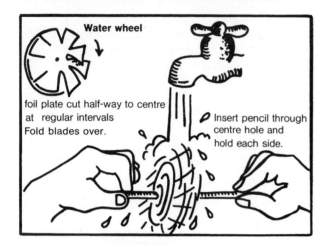

Water wheel

foil plate cut half-way to centre at regular intervals
Fold blades over.

Insert pencil through centre hole and hold each side.

Copymasters

Use copymaster 21 (Water pushes things) to record this activity. This can be done as a class demonstration with the teacher holding the hose pipe or other jet. Use the objects shown as they represent a variety of sizes, shapes and materials. Try each in turn and record the results afterwards.

Ask the children why they think some objects move along better than others and why some objects do not move at all even though small and light e.g. the feather and the paper which may become sodden quickly.

Attainment target 11: Electricity and magnetism

Pupils should develop their knowledge and understanding of electric and electromagnetic effects in simple circuits, electric devices and domestic appliances.

Level 1

Statements of attainment

Pupils should:

- know that many household appliances use electricity but that misuse could be dangerous.

Area of study 1

WHAT IS ELECTRICITY?

C22

Purpose
To identify different types of electricity.

Materials needed
Balloons, combs, paper, Cellophane, photographs of fork lightning, ball lightning, sheet lightning; baking tray, Plasticine®, large plastic bag, tin lid.

Activity 1
Discuss different types of electricity using photographs.

Activity 2: Static electricity experiments
Blow up a balloon and rub it vigorously on the hair or on a jumper, then hold it just above the hair. The friction should have produced enough static electricity to make the hair stand on end. Rub the balloon again and hold it against the wall or the ceiling. It should stick to these surfaces for some time.

Activity 3: Fishing game
This is another static electricity experiment. Cut out some small fish shapes (about 6 cm long) from tissue paper, and put them on the table. Use the comb to comb the hair vigorously for about 30 seconds then place the comb near the fish. They should fly up to it, attracted by the static electricity. This works best with dry, clean hair.

A game can be made by attaching the comb to a home-made fishing rod and using a small PE hoop as a pond.

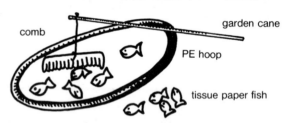

comb

garden cane

PE hoop

tissue paper fish

Activity 4: Make a spark of lightning
You will need the baking tray, lump of Plasticine®, large plastic bag and the tin lid to do this.

Press the piece of Plasticine® on to the middle of the baking tray so that it sticks well. Then put the tray down on to the plastic bag, hold the lump of Plasticine® and rub the tray round and round. Now pick up the tray by the Plasticine®. Hold something metal, such as a small tin lid, against one corner and you should see a big spark jump from the tray to the lid (see illustration on page 21). This is most effective in a darkened room.

Explain to the children that tiny amounts of electricity can be made by rubbing certain things together and that these tiny and often invisible sparks, such as are produced in the balloon experiment, are not dangerous, but that larger amounts of electricity can be very dangerous.

Copymasters

Use copymaster 22 (Static electricity) to make a collection of things which *can* be picked up by static electricity. Allow the children to experiment with materials which are attracted by static and those which are not. Include the things on the sheet. Use small pieces only as the amount of static produced by a balloon or comb is very small and although small pieces of a material will be attracted, larger pieces of the same material may prove too heavy. The pieces of attractable material can then be stuck on the sheet in the appropriate place to provide a record.

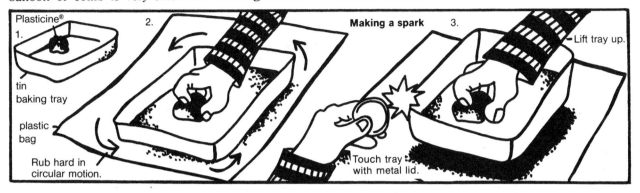

Plasticine®
1.
tin
baking tray
plastic bag
Rub hard in circular motion.
2.
Making a spark 3.
Lift tray up.
Touch tray with metal lid.

USING ELECTRICITY

Area of study 2

C23

Purpose

To identify ways in which electricity is used in home and school.

Materials needed

Mail order catalogues, catalogues of electrical equipment, educational catalogues (such as Yorkshire Purchasing Organisation or Nottingham Educational Supplies catalogues of school equipment), scissors, glue and paper, small battery, light bulb and plastic covered fine wire.

Activity 1

Make the point that electricity can exist as huge sparks as in lightning or tiny ones as in the balloon experiment and that these sparks jump to earth. Electricity can also be made to travel along pathways of metal, i.e. wires. To prove this on a small scale set up a simple circuit with a light bulb, battery and two pieces of wire. Show that when the pathway is broken the electricity does not reach the bulb to light it.

Activity 2

Take a walk around the school and observe and discuss which appliances and machines use electricity, e.g. lights, kettles, record players. Go into the school kitchen and look at the machines used there. Discuss how the machines are attached to the power source and search for the socket used for each.

Make sure that the children know that they should never touch these sockets, loaded or unloaded and that only adults are allowed to plug machines into the power source. Many accidents are caused when young children insert plugs with damp or wet hands. You should make the points that electricity can travel through their bodies because they have water in their

tissues, that this mains electricity is much more powerful than that from a little battery and that it can kill them.

Activity 2

Make a photo collection of the machines that you found by searching through the catalogues. The children can try to cut out the photographs themselves and place them in the correct room on a large cross-sectional picture of the school. By placing the words next to the picture, vocabulary can also be built up (see overleaf).

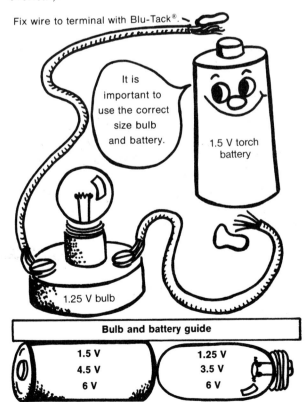

Fix wire to terminal with Blu-Tack®.

It is important to use the correct size bulb and battery.

1.5 V torch battery

1.25 V bulb

Bulb and battery guide	
1.5 V	1.25 V
4.5 V	3.5 V
6 V	6 V

Write room name in red and vocabulary in black.

Put pictures and vocabulary in the correct room.

We found all these electrical things in our school.

Hall — light

Office — typewriter, computer, photocopier

Kitchen — food mixer, micro-wave, kettle

Classroom — computer, radio, light, calculator

record player, alarm, video recorder, television, slide projector

Caretaker's room — polisher, vacuum

Copymasters

Use copymaster 23 (Electrical appliances at home) to record observations in this activity. This sheet is a cross section of a home showing four rooms: kitchen/dining room, lounge, bedroom and bathroom. Children can search through the catalogues for the different appliances which they have at home. They can then select one or two appliances for each room and stick them on the sheet. Allow them to draw in the lead, plug and socket for each. Take this opportunity to reiterate the safety rules.

Area of study 3

MISUSE OF ELECTRICITY

C24

Purpose

To identify dangers in the misuse of electrical appliances and equipment.

Materials needed

Photographs of hydro-electric, coal and oil fired power stations, the Central Electricity Generating Board video: 'Play safe'. (This video is sometimes considered frightening for young children, possibly due to its highly dramatic presentation rather than any horrific visuals. But we feel it makes a very effective point about the dangers of playing near potential sources of danger, and if viewing is sensitively prepared and followed up then it is suitable for infants.)

Activity 1

Walk round the school and look at the ways in which electricity is used. Be on the look out for faulty wires, worn and old appliances, and sockets overloaded with too many adaptors and plugs. Talk about the danger of misuse, i.e. fire hazard or electrocution and burns. Talk about not touching hotplates on cookers or poking fingers into sockets. Stress that children should never touch any part of an electrical appliance with wet hands because electricity can travel along a path of water.

Activity 2

Go for a walk around the local neighbourhood and look for pylons and sub-stations. Talk about the dangers of playing near the electrical supply. Explain that apart from the fact that electricity can travel along a pathway of water or metal it can also jump quite long distances as huge sparks. For example children should never fly kites near overhead lines because damp air may wet the kite string and provide a conductor.

Show pictures of the different types of power stations and make the point that these places are where we make electricity for our use. Electricity such as that in lightning is not man-made but created by natural forces.

Watch the Central Electricity Generating Board's video 'Play safe'.

Copymasters

Use copymaster 24 (Dangers from electricity) to consolidate learning in this activity. Use the picture to identify misuse of electrical appliances in the home. The children have to circle the things which may be dangerous.

Attainment target 12: The scientific aspects of information technology including microelectronics

Pupils should develop their knowledge and understanding of information transfer and microelectronics.

| Level **1** | **Statements of attainment** |

Pupils should:

- know about some everyday devices which receive text, sound and images over long distances, using information technology.

Area of study 1

ENTERTAINMENT

 C25

Purpose
To identify those everyday devices which receive signals, images and text for the purpose of entertainment.

Materials needed
TV (with Teletext) and radios (a variety of makes and sizes, e.g. personal stereo/radio with headphones), mail order and store catalogues with photos of these items in the widest variety.

Activity 1
Discuss the notion of entertainment on TV and radio. It will be fairly difficult to make the distinction between those programmes beamed out on TV or radio and the seemingly same items enjoyed on video or audio cassette. The simplest idea involves telling the children that video and audio cassettes are like books and records which we can watch and listen to any time we want because the programme is stored on them, but that the TV and radio programmes are specially sent out from the stations at certain times. You may want to do Activity 3 at this point.

Activity 2
Watch a TV or listen to a radio programme (see the *Radio Times*) which can either be a schools' programme or some other. Make sure it is entertaining. Make the point to the children that entertainment is something we do for relaxation and enjoyment and that in the case of TV and radio we are fairly passive. We tend only to look and listen. If you can, show the children the Teletext facility on a TV which has entertainment items such as a jokes section.

Activity 3
Other forms of entertainment do not need these technological machines. You can discuss what other pastimes the children enjoy, perhaps dividing them into those which need a special machine (computer, Scalextric, radio-controlled cars) and those which do not (ball games, chasing games, hide and seek).

Activity 4
Take a class census of favourite TV programmes and make a pictogram to find the most popular. Use standard size paper and get the children to draw one character from the programme to represent it.

Activity 5
Look through the catalogues for pictures of as many different TVs and radios as possible. As part of the always valuable cutting and sticking exercise, cut them out and make two sets. Try to find as great a variety as you can from the miniature wrist TV to the wall-mounted TV screen and from the huge 'ghetto-blasters' to the tiny personal stereo radios. If possible display some of these items for a day.

Copymasters
Use copymaster 25 (My favourite TV programme) to record this activity. The children can draw a character or a scene from the programme on the screen section and in the space below they can name the programme or write a short piece about it, e.g. 'My favourite TV programme is "Fireman Sam". I like it because Norman is naughty.'

Area of study 2

COMMUNICATION

 C26

Purpose

To identify those everyday devices which receive signals, images and text for the purposes of communication.

Materials needed

TV (with Teletext), radio, telephone, CB radio, intercom system, baby alarm. (It may be difficult to borrow these items so magazine or catalogue pictures can serve instead.)

Activity 1

Discuss the idea of two-way communication with someone a long way away, made possible by use of a special machine. You will also need to discuss one-way communication as when information is passed from source to a watcher or listener who does not need to respond, as when we watch the news or a factual programme on TV or use the Teletext facility. Sometimes it is possible to respond, for example with TV phone-ins. Show the children the items and ideally allow them to hold and use them.

Activity 2

Watch and listen to items such as the weather forecast, extracts from the news and adverts. Select Teletext TV programme forecasts, adverts, news and recipes for the children to see the extent of the facility.

Activity 3

Install toy or old telephones in the home corner for the children to use in their play. Add pretend wires, a telephone directory and a notepad and pencil to extend the play by enlarging the idea of communications.

Activity 4

As for 'Entertainment', search the commercial catalogues for a variety of pictures of different communications devices ranging from baby alarms and car phones to novelty telephones and intercoms.

Activity 5

If you can, arrange to take small groups of children to the local telephone box and explain its use. This could provide an experience some children have never had. Perhaps a helper or the school secretary could man the school phone for a short period whilst you put through a call with the children. Make a call box in your home corner and show the children how to make a 999 call, but stress the importance of never using this on a real phone unless there is a genuine emergency.

Copymasters

Use copymaster 26 (Talking to someone a long way away) to record this activity. This sheet shows a variety of devices used for communication and entertainment. The children have to find among these the items used to contact another person.

 Area of study 3

ENVIRONMENTAL SIGNS

 C27

Purpose

To identify devices in the local environment which transmit and receive sound and image signals.

Materials needed

Catalogue pictures of aerials and satellite dishes, photos of radio masts and TV transmitters, card, glue, pens, small model houses.

Activity 1

Make a simple and quick model of the layout of the TV transmission network: use quick drawings or cut out photos of aerials and masts and two buildings, stick these to card tubes or small boxes and add milk bottle tops for transmitters.

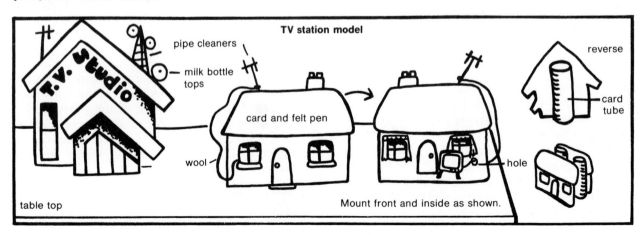

TV station model — pipe cleaners — milk bottle tops — card and felt pen — wool — table top — reverse — card tube — hole — Mount front and inside as shown.

Explain at a very simple level that the signals are beamed through the air and caught by the TV aerial, travel down the wire and into the aerial socket on the TV. You could demonstrate how the picture is lost if the aerial is disconnected.

Stress how important it is that the children never touch these electrical sockets themselves and especially with damp hands.

Photocopy, enlarge and display near sockets.

Activity 2

Show the children the pictures of the different devices, then go out into the playground or walk round school and look for examples. Depending on your school location it may be possible to spot transmitters and receivers on police, fire and ambulance stations, on local beacons and hills, taxi control offices and indeed TV stations. Look for smaller aerials on houses, cars, motor bikes and boats. Try to spot telegraph poles and wires and their source.

Copymasters

Use copymaster 27 (I spy aerials) to record work in this activity. The sheet shows a street scene with several different devices in location. The children have to circle these and count them.

Attainment target 13: Energy

Pupils should develop their knowledge and understanding of the nature of energy, its transfer and control.

They should develop their knowledge and understanding of the range of energy sources and the issues involved in their exploitation.

Statements of attainment

Pupils should:

● understand that they need food to be active.
● be able to describe, by talking or other appropriate means, how food is necessary for life.

 CAREFUL EATING

C28

Area of study 1

Purpose

To show that careful eating is necessary to stay active.

Materials needed

Photo montage pictures of complete meals for classroom display, photo montage of children's favourite meals, a selection of packets and tins from various types of food and drink.

Activity 1

Identify those foods which are healthy foods. Make the point that a little of each kind of food is better for the body than an excess of fatty foods, cakes and sweets.

Activity 2

Discuss what can happen if the children eat too much of one thing, i.e. that it can lead to sickness and feeling ill.

Activity 3

Ask the children to describe the kinds of foods they like to eat and why. Ask them to consider what it would be like if they could eat only the thing they liked best, for example chocolate, all day and every day.

Copymasters

Use copymaster 28 (We are what we eat) for the children to record the facts about careful eating. Children are to draw a coloured circle round the foods which give us energy (the fatty and starchy foods), those which are body building (the high protein foods) and those which help to clean out the body (the high fibre foods).

FOOD FOR ENERGY

C29

Purpose
To show that we need to eat different kinds of food for energy.

Materials needed
Samples of energy giving foods for the children to try: fruit, vegetables, bread, butter, jam, syrup (if necessary allow for ethnic variations), a variety of fresh and processed foods, the same photo montage pictures recommended for 'Careful eating' on page 25.

Activity 1
Arrange samples of food and let the children taste each of the samples. Discuss why they chose a particular food first. Was it because of the colour, taste or smell?

Activity 2
Discuss the different types of food that we usually eat at breakfast, lunch, evening meal and supper. Children can compile their own cut-out favourite meals from the magazine photos and stick them on to a paper plate. Talk about ethnic differences in food preference.

Activity 3
Try to discover which foods give us most energy. Show the children how to identify fatty foods, starchy foods

and those with lots of fibre, by feeling the texture, taste and appearance. Point out that too many fatty foods can lead to heart disease and stress the importance of a balanced diet to overall health. Give them simple facts such as:

- Bread, cereals and fats give us warmth and energy.
- Meat gives us protein which helps to build up muscles.
- Sugar gives us energy.
- Vitamins and minerals help the body to work properly.
- Fibre helps to clean out the body.

Copymasters
Use copymaster 29 (The food we eat) to show the kinds of food the children ought to eat at different times of the day in order to achieve a balanced diet. It could also be used to show the children's favourite foods. They could draw in their favourite food for each meal or stick pictures on the plates. (See also *Blueprints: Topics* in this series for a topic on food.)

FOOD FOR LIFE

C30

Purpose
To show that without food living things die.

Materials needed
RSPCA photographs of maltreated animals (chosen with care so as not to cause distress to younger children), a selection of different animal and plant foods such as tinned dog food, budgie seed, fish food, sunflower seeds, plant fertiliser for comparison with the foods we eat; photographs from world charity organisations of famine and hunger in the Third World to show the effect of lack of proper nourishment in human beings.

Activity 1
Look at the pictures of humans and animals and talk about the obvious effects of hunger. Discuss what the children themselves feel like when they are hungry.

Activity 2
Talk about drought and famine. A small assembly could be arranged for the school with a possible link to harvest time. (See also in this series, *Blueprints: Assemblies* for an assembly on autumn and harvest.)

Activity 3
Use the different kinds of animal and plant foods to illustrate a discussion on the needs of the various plants and animals; for example, budgies do not eat meat and dogs do not eat millet seed.

Activity 4
Set up a very simple experiment with sunflower seeds. Plant three pots of seeds. Water one pot solely with water and one with regular feeds of plant food. Leave the third totally without water and food. Discuss the results.

Copymasters
Use copymaster 30 (All living things need food) to record this activity. It is a simple cross-mapping exercise to show the different kinds of food eaten by animals. It also makes the point that living things need water.

Attainment target 14: Sound and music

Pupils should develop their knowledge and understanding of the properties, transmission and absorption of sound.

Level 1

Statements of attainment

Pupils should:

● know that sounds can be made in a variety of ways.

Area of study 1

MAKING SOUND WITH THE VOICE

C31

Purpose
To show that voices can make a variety of different sounds.

Materials needed
The children's voices; tape recordings or records of different types of adult voices (gruff, bell-like, deep, resonant and so on) – recordings could be spoken or sung; recordings of different adults and children around school; recordings of different common animal voices (dog, horse, cow, sheep, chicken, blackbird, guinea pig) – you may be also able to get more uncommon ones such as the sounds of zoo animals (lion, seal, camel, peacock, dolphin); pictures of the animals on your recording.

Activity 1
Have a guessing game. Play the recorded animal voices and ask the children to identify them. You could make a visual aid and vocabulary sheet by displaying the animal pictures with the appropriate sound word, for example 'woof', 'miaow'.

What do these animals say ?

I	say	moo
I	say	woof
I	say	miaow
I	say	cluck
I	say	baa

Activity 2
Play a similar guessing game with the voices of people in school to see if the children can identify them.

Activity 3
Make recordings of the children speaking and then try to get them to make as many different sounds with the voice as possible, for example, whispering, talking, shouting, humming, clicking, whistling, groaning, pretending to cry.

The children can also try to imitate the animal sounds. Get them to try to vary the pitch and tone of the sounds, sometimes making very soft sounds and sometimes very loud ones, then hard sounds, bubbling sounds, long thin sounds and so on.

Activity 4
Talk about rhythm in sounds. Mention natural rhythms such as the patter of raindrops or the clopping of a horse's hooves. They can try to imitate these with the voice. Get the children to speak their names and help them to recognise the rhythm in the names, for example, 'Jennifer' has three syllables, 'Tom' has one. Some names have a longer emphasis on one or more of the syllables, for example, 'Charlie' has one long and one short sound. Make up a sound pattern with several children chanting their names together, like a singing round.

Activity 5
Sing any of the songs the children enjoy.

Activity 6
Make a sound story. Tell one of the children's favourite stories and get them to add the sound effects using their voices, e.g., 'The little red hen' story. The children could make the sound of the hen pouring the ingredients into her bowl, beating the mixture, banging the oven door and so on.

Copymasters

Use copymaster 31 (Downy duckling's walk) to consolidate this activity. The children can follow the words of the story with you and every time there is a picture, they make a sound associated with what it represents.

 ## MAKING SOUND WITH INSTRUMENTS

Area of study 2   C32

Purpose

To show that a variety of sounds can be made with musical instruments.

Materials needed

Milk bottles, old spoons, metal bottle tops, an old broom handle, coffee tins, washing-up liquid bottles, yoghurt cartons, small cardboard boxes, a variety of rubber bands, assorted plastic tubing, cardboard tubes, combs, paper, pens, glue, Sellotape, paint, PVA glue, an old washing-up bowl, an old shoe box with lid, thick string, art straws, sandpaper, odd pieces of wood, thick uncovered wire, 'real' musical instruments, with examples of the three categories of sound production, i.e.:

a) Banging: all tuned and untuned percussion instruments
b) Plucking: guitar, ukulele, harp
c) Blowing: recorder, kazoo, Swannee whistle, trumpet, flute, etc.

Activity 1

Explore the 'real' instruments, one category at a time, discussing how the sound is produced, what it sounds like and what feelings or impressions it produces. Give

the children plenty of practice with each instrument. Display them in your music corner in the categories already mentioned (see below).

Activity 2

Make musical instruments. The children will learn a great deal about the behaviour of materials and the nature of sound from an activity of this kind.

Activity 3

Make a sound story, this time using the real or the made instruments to illustrate the action, e.g. maracas for the sound of rain falling, pan lid cymbals for lightning, drums for thunder, sand in a long tube for the sound of water running, etc.

Copymasters

Use copymaster 32 (How I made a sound on this instrument?). It is a simple sorting and classifying exercise in which the children have to decide how they made the sound with each instrument. Join the instrument to the correct source.

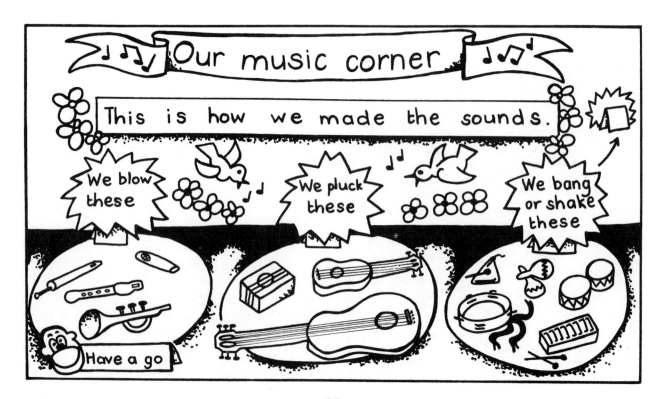

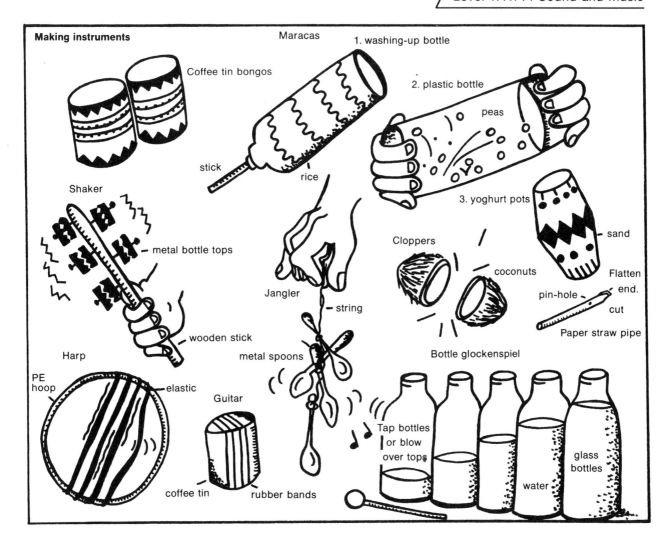

Making instruments

Maracas

1. washing-up bottle

Coffee tin bongos

2. plastic bottle

peas

stick

rice

3. yoghurt pots

Shaker

sand

metal bottle tops

Cloppers

coconuts

Flatten end.

Jangler

pin-hole

cut

wooden stick

string

Paper straw pipe

Harp

metal spoons

Bottle glockenspiel

PE hoop

elastic

Guitar

Tap bottles or blow over tops

glass bottles

coffee tin

rubber bands

water

| Area of study 3 | **SOUNDS IN THE ENVIRONMENT** | C33 |

Purpose
To show that the world around us is full of a great variety of sounds made by many things.

Materials needed
A tape recorder, tape of common household sounds (e.g. tap running, door banging, telephone ringing or buzzing, car engine starting, washing machine working, vacuum cleaner working, liquid poured from a bottle, a crisp packet being screwed up, zipping up a coat), an assortment of blindfolds, e.g. scarves.

Activity 1
Hold a listening game in the classroom. Blindfold six children at once and let the others take it in turns to make a noise in the room for them to guess, for example, scrape a chair along the floor, open a cupboard, shake a pencil box, etc.

Activity 2
Take a walk around school and see how many noises you can hear. Try to guess the origin of each sound. Either take the tape recorder with you to record your findings or make a list yourself as you go round. Try to discover: the quietest place in school; the noisiest place in school; the quietest time in school; the noisiest time in school.

Activity 3
Have a sound quiz. Play the tape of common household sounds to two teams. The team which guesses the most is the winner.

Activity 4
If possible go for a walk around the neighbourhood. Record the sound of machines that make a noise, and natural sounds such as the wind, rain, sound of the trees, etc.

Copymasters
Use copymaster 33 (Sounds) to consolidate learning on this activity. Working with the teacher, the children have to put the sounds in order of loudness. You will need to have these sounds taped as you will have to play them several times.

29

Attainment target 15: Using light and electromagnetic radiation

Pupils should develop their knowledge and understanding of the properties and behaviour of light and electromagnetic waves.

Statements of attainment

Pupils should:

- know that light comes from different sources.
- be able to discriminate between colours and match them or, where appropriate, demonstrate an understanding of colour in the environment.

WHERE DOES LIGHT COME FROM?

Purpose
To identify sources of light: natural and man-made.

Materials needed
Pictures of the Sun and Moon, lightning storms, electrical and gas lights and light from fires; a collection of different kinds of lights and some candles, pictures of different kinds of lights which are not available for display, e.g. chandeliers, wall lights, standard lights, desk lights, car headlights, light-houses.

Activity 1
Identify the sources of light, i.e. the Sun, electricity and fire. Take a look around the classroom and try to spot the light sources there.

Activity 2
Look around the outside of school and in the streets around. Look at street lighting, signs on shops, car headlights, porch lights, kiosk lights.

Activity 3
Talk about the light at night. The Moon reflects the Sun, and stars twinkle in the sky. Ask the children to look for ways we use lights at night, i.e. in houses and on the street to advertise, warn, guide, etc.

Activity 4
Talk about the light generated by electrical storms and power stations.

Copymasters
Use copymaster 34 (Lights) to record observations in this activity. The children can look out for the various types of light as they walk round the neighbourhood in the day or at night. They then have to circle the light sources on the picture.

IDENTIFYING AND MIXING COLOURS

Purpose
To recognise that the colours in the environment are made up of different tones and shades.

Materials needed
Paints, pictures of people from different ethnic groups and if possible people with different coloured hair, skin and eyes, a range of natural objects, for example, fruits and vegetables for extracting natural dyes, food colourings, coloured lights for a Christmas tree, filter paper and Smarties or felt pens, card and wool or embroidery cotton.

Activity 1
Use paints in the primary colours (red, blue, yellow) and also black and white and let the children

experiment with mixing. Let them mix two colours and then add black or white to get different shades and tones.

Activity 2
Look at pictures of different racial types and discuss colour of skin, hair and eyes in the class.

Activity 3
Take a selection of natural objects, e.g. onions or beetroot, bark or coffee. Boil them in a pan of water one at a time to make a natural dye. Children can try to guess what colour of dye will be produced. Test by soaking a piece of white cotton material in the dye and then let it dry.

Remember that an adult should always be present when water is heated. Temperatures lower than boiling point can scald young children.

Activity 4
Experiment with different food colourings on everyday foods, for example, blue fish fingers, red cornflakes, orange peas, etc. Discuss with the children how they would feel if their favourite foods were different colours.

Activity 5
Experiment with chromatography. Take a piece of filter paper and place a Smartie sweet in the centre. Drop one drop of water on to it. The sugar coating will dissolve, releasing the dyes which colour the sweet. Some colours dissolve faster than others and are deposited on the filter paper nearer the centre of the sweet. Others are carried in suspension further away from the centre, so that a bull's eye of colours is produced. You will find that each colour sweet has its own combination of colours in the dye.

Alternatively, this experiment can be carried out using felt-tip pens instead of Smarties. Put a one centimetre dot of felt pen colour and a drop of water as before in the centre of the filter paper.

Activity 6: Make a spinner
Cut a circle of card and make two holes in it. Thread wool or embroidery cotton through the holes and tie in a loop. Colour the card with sections of different colours to show, when the card is spun, that these colours blend together to make white. If two colours only are used then these two will mix, i.e. red and blue to make purple.

The two loops are held in each hand and the spinner tossed over and over until the wool on each side is tightly twisted. Pull each hand apart gently to make the spinner spin and blend the colours.

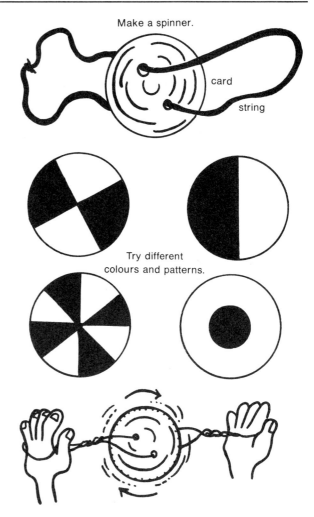

Make a spinner.

card
string

Try different colours and patterns.

Copymasters
Use copymaster 35 (Mixing colours) to consolidate learning on this activity. The children need to recognise primary colours. The exercise involves them actually mixing colours on the page.

Area of study 3
COLOURS IN THE ENVIRONMENT
 C36

Purpose
To show that colour is associated with certain things: camouflage, danger and display.

Materials needed
A collection of pictures of flowers, insects, snakes and other animals which use one of these three features very obviously, pictures of signs and signals.

Activity 1
Display the pictures of brightly coloured creatures and flowers and talk about the reasons why colour is so important.

Activity 2
Discuss camouflage and the use of patterns of colour, e.g. zebra and giraffe; colour for safety, etc.

Activity 3
Talk about colours used for warnings, e.g. on certain poisonous plants and creatures. Sometimes nature uses trickery and gives an animal a 'danger colour' when it is not poisonous so that colouring becomes a safety feature for that animal.

Activity 4
Talk about colour used for display or attraction. Plants have beautifully coloured flowers to attract insects. Some animals, such as peacocks, are very brightly coloured to attract a mate.

Activity 5
Look at the pictures of road signs and traffic lights: red for danger or stop, green for go. Include discussion of the Green Cross Code.

Activity 6

Talk about the children's favourite colours and how colours make them feel. You can discuss the colours used to decorate school or the children's homes, particularly their bedrooms. The children could paint a picture of their favourite coloured things.

Activity 7

Paint a huge rainbow for the wall and let the children paint their own.

Copymasters

Use copymaster 36 (Colours in nature) to identify the colour in the environment. Children choose the correct colours usually associated with the areas to be coloured, e.g. blue-tone sky, white clouds, green grass. The activity is open-ended to allow for local and seasonal variations, such as 'The sky was red last night' or 'My tree has orange leaves because it is autumn' or 'Our grass is yellow because it is very dry'.

Attainment target 16: The Earth in space

Pupils should develop their knowledge and understanding of the relative positions and movement of the Earth, Moon, Sun and of the solar system within the universe.

Level 1

Statements of attainment

Pupils should:

- be able to describe through talking, or other appropriate means, the seasonal changes that occur in the weather and in living things.
- know the danger of looking directly at the Sun.
- be able to describe, in relation to their home or school, the apparent daily motion of the Sun across the sky.

Area of study 1

THE SEASONS

C37

Purpose

To identify the four seasons of the year.

Materials needed

A collection of pictures to show the changes which occur during the four seasons; a selection of clothes worn during the different seasons, seeds, berries, leaves, etc. or whatever seasonal plants are available at the time; poems and stories about the seasons.

Activity 1

Look at the seasonal pictures and compare similarities and differences, drawing upon the children's own reminiscences of things they have done at different times of the year. Put the pictures in order, starting at the beginning of the year.

Activity 2

Make a seasonal clock using some of the pictures stuck in the appropriate quadrant.

Activity 3

If possible visit a farm and look at the seasonal jobs which are in progress.

Talk about other jobs which are done at different times of the year in and around our homes and gardens, for example, spring cleaning, raking up the leaves, planting bulbs, clearing away snow, putting in bedding plants.

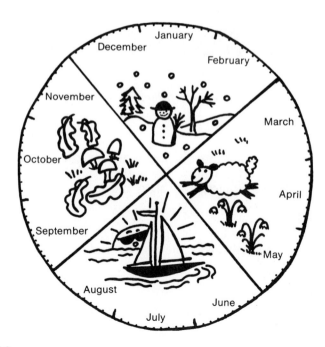

Activity 4
Make a linear frieze of the jobs done at different times of the year and another to show the fun activities associated with the seasons, for example, flying kites, bonfires, fireworks, paddling pools, snow fights, building snowmen.

Copymasters
Use copymaster 37 (The seasons). Get the children to draw themselves in each box, wearing the appropriate clothes and engaged in whatever activity they like to do at that time of the year. You can photocopy the top and bottom halves separately and enlarge them to A4 size to give more room to draw in, if necessary.

PLANTS AND ANIMALS

Purpose
To look at changes in plant and animal life during the four seasons of the year.

Materials needed
Books and pictures of plant and animal life, pictures of animals that hibernate and migrate, seasonal pictures of plants and trees, pictures of baby animals such as tadpoles, lambs, rabbits, foals, baby birds, etc. seeds, bulbs and plants which are available at the time, bird-table, wildlife videos showing migration and hibernation of British wildlife, if possible some live eggs and an incubator for hatching in the classroom.

Activity 1
Set up a bird-table. Observe, identify and record the birds which visit. Pay particular attention to the bird-table in winter and make sure there is a good supply of assorted foods and water. This observation and recording could be done by different groups of children through the year and a comparison made at the end of the differences in bird life between the seasons.

The details can be recorded on a simple sheet.

We spotted these birds in the Autumn.						
bird	number					
robin	1	2	3	4	5	
blackbird	1	2	3			
wren	1	2				
starling	1					
thrush	1	2	3			

Activity 2
Make a bird cake from assorted seeds, apples, stale cake, nuts and half a pound of lard.

Melt the lard, mix in the seeds and break up the cake into breadcrumb consistency. Mix well and leave to cool slightly. Pour into an old margarine tub and put a length of string into the mixture, leaving one end to hang over the edge of the tub. When set hard remove from the tub and use the string to hang the cake in a place safe from cats.

Activity 3
Talk about migration and why some birds fly south for the winter. Also mention the birds which actually come to this country for the winter such as Canada geese.

Activity 4
Talk about hibernation and why some creatures sleep for the winter. If possible try to link this with the seasonal changes in the weather. Explore the school grounds and neighbourhood for suitable places for different animals to hibernate.

Look at frogs, toads, squirrels, bats and dormice. Talk about the seasonal changes which occur in their natural habitats.

Activity 5
Depending on the season, gather or collect lots of different examples of plant life.

In spring: grow bulbs and compare rates of growth and size and shape. Compare similarities and differences between plants and trees.

In summer: look at the profusion of flowers and talk about the wide range of plants. Compare size, shape and colour of petals and leaves.

In autumn: look at trees which lose their leaves, the changing colours, the feel and smell of the plants as their leaves decay and die. Look at fungi and berries.

In winter: look at tree shapes, bark patterns and textures. Find out which plants grow all through the winter months and discuss why there is a slowing down of plant growth at this time of the year: you may ask 'Does the lawn need to be cut as often during the winter?'

Activity 6

Talk about the way the seasons affect our bodies. How do we keep warm? Talk about clothes and the remedies we take to protect ourselves from the seasons, e.g. adding extra clothes or wearing cool, thin, cotton clothes, wearing sun protection creams or waterproof clothes to keep us dry.

Copymasters

Use copymaster 38 (Changes in living things) to identify these seasonal changes. The children match up the pictures with the seasons and then complete the words in the centre.

 Area of study 3

SHADOWS

 C39

Purpose

To look at the apparent daily motion of the Sun across the sky.

Materials needed

Scissors, black activity paper, chalk, powder paint, poems and songs, for example, 'Me and my shadow'.

Activity 1

Look around the classroom and observe through which window the Sun is shining, which parts of the classroom are in sunshine and which are in shade. Do this several times during the day from a spot marked on the floor. Plot the movement of the Sun by painting a tiny Sun on the window at the key times.

Before this activity talk about the danger of looking directly at the Sun.

Activity 2

Go out into the playground and play shadow patterns as a group or with the whole class. Let the children try shadow boxing and jumping on each other's shadows.

Activity 3

Cast a child's shadow on black activity paper. The teacher can draw around it with chalk and the children

can help to cut it out. Choose two children, one large and one small for comparison.

Activity 4

Make a shadow clock. Mark a cross on a suitable place in the playground where no other shadows fall. A child can stand on the spot and the teacher draws round the shadow at several times during the day, possibly early morning, playtime, lunch time, and just before home time. Discuss why the length of the shadow varies.

Activity 5

Ask the children to make some observations at home. Let them find out which side of the house the Sun shines on in the morning, at lunch time, in the afternoon and evening. Ask them to discover the sunniest room in the house and at what time in the day it is at its sunniest.

Copymasters

Use copymaster 39 (Shadows) to record work on this activity. The children are to look at the position of the sun and try to draw in the shadow at the right place. Do this as practically as possible by setting up the event in the playground so that the children can observe at first hand exactly where the shadow falls.

Mark a spot in the playground and draw round your shadow there at different times of the day.

9 o'clock   12 o'clock   3 o'clock

Making shadow creatures   Moving shadows

LEVEL 2

Attainment target 1: Exploration of science

Pupils should develop the intellectual and practical skills that allow them to explore the world of science and to develop a fuller understanding of scientific phenomena and the procedures of scientific exploration and investigation. This work should take place in the context of activities that require a progressively more systematic and quantified approach, which draws upon an increasing knowledge and understanding of science. The activities should encourage the ability to:

i.   plan, hypothesise and predict
ii. design and carry out investigations
iii. interpret results and findings
iv. draw inferences
v.   communicate exploratory tasks and experiments.

Level 2

Statements of attainment

Pupils should:

- ask questions and suggest ideas of the 'how', 'why', and 'what will happen if' variety.
- identify simple differences, for example, *hot/cold, rough/smooth.*
- use non-standard and standard measures, for example, *hand-spans and rulers.*
- list and collate observations.
- interpret findings by associating one factor with another, for example, the pupils' perception at this level that 'light objects float', 'thin wood is bendy'.
- record findings in charts, drawings and other appropriate forms.

As the children are working on the activities at this Level they will have the opportunity to do work contributing to AT1 as the activities in the text are all designed to do this. For example, in AT6 (Types and uses of materials), Area of Study 1, Activity 1, the children are sorting and classifying different materials and collating the information on a chart, thus satisfying the requirements of AT1 as they will be asking questions, identifying differences, recording and collating findings and attempting to interpret those findings.

A bar code of symbols relating to AT1 has been created and below is the key to it.

The full bar code appears on the record sheet to help you record the children's experiences. These symbols, which are linked to work on the copymasters, appear in the text at the appropriate place.

Observation	Discussion	Ask questions	Identify	Measure	List	Record findings	Interpret findings

Attainment target 2: The variety of life

Pupils should develop their knowledge and understanding of the diversity and classification of past and present life-forms, and of the relationships, energy flows, cycles of matter and human influences within ecosystems.

Level 2

Statements of attainment

Pupils should:

- know that plants and animals need certain conditions to sustain life.
- understand how living things are looked after and be able to treat them with care and consideration.

Area of study 1 — WHAT PLANTS NEED TO LIVE

C40

Purpose
To identify the conditions plants need to sustain life.

Materials needed
Pictures, photographs and videos of the many different places plants can grow (look at plants which grow in desert lands, mountains, jungles, ponds and rivers, polar regions, on the sea bed, on tundra and in the local environment); a selection of different plants (include cacti, succulents, ivies, ferns, underwater plants, flowering house plants); growing mediums, containers (small dishes, bulb jars), shoe box, mustard and cress seed, cotton wool.

Activity 1
Display the pictures and posters and watch the videos. Talk about the kind of plants which grow in the different regions and locations shown. Discuss with the children the similarities and differences between plants which grow in a particular environment, for example: Do only cacti grow in the desert? Are they all the same shape? Do they all have sharp needles? What do you think the needles are there for?

Compare plants from other locations and talk about similarities and differences between the different groups.

Think about things plants need in order to grow well. Do all plants need water?

Activity 2
Set up a simple experiment with two of the plants. Water one regularly and stop watering the other one completely. Ask the children what they think will happen. They can make their own observations over a period of time and you can help them to form conclusions.

Other questions might include: How much water shall we give to the plant? What will happen if we give it too much water? How can we be sure we have given the same amount of water each day? Should the plants be of the same species? How could we measure if the watered plant has grown? It may be necessary to sacrifice one of the plants in order to observe the effects of non-watering.

The children could set up an experiment to show that some plants can go for a long time without water while others will wilt and die in a very short time.

Activity 3
Look at the way plants take water through their roots and stems. Growing hyacinth or daffodil bulbs in bulb jars will show reasonably quickly how a root system develops when the bulb is exposed to moisture. Keep one bulb dry as a control, so that the children can see that if the bulb does not have water it will not grow.

A simple experiment to show how plants take water up through their stems can be undertaken with a stick of celery placed in a jar of water coloured with ink.

As the celery takes up the coloured water the stalk will change colour. The same experiment can be done with white carnations, to colour the flower.

Activity 4: Do all plants need light?

The green leaves of a plant trap energy by using sunlight in a process called photosynthesis. If light is restricted then the plant will not grow well. Use mustard and cress seed to illustrate this. Get two shallow dishes and place in each a layer of cotton wool which you should then soak with water.

Spread seeds thinly on each. Put one dish on a sunny window sill and the other in a dark place. Keep both well watered and observe the different rates of growth after germination.

An extension of this, to show the powerful effect of light, is to put one dish of seeds in a shoe box with a lid. First cut a hole in one end of the box and put the seed dish at the other end. Keep the dish watered but put the lid on the box. After a few days remove the lid. Ask the children to suggest why the seedlings look like this. Can the children think of another way to make the seedlings bend?

Children could also look around school to see if they can see any other plants which are bending towards a light source. Do all plants need the same amount of light? Look at ferns and other shade-loving plants.

What do the children think will happen if they get too much sun?

Activity 5: Do plants need warmth?

Using the mustard and cress seeds in dishes of cotton wool as before, place one dish on a warm, sunny window sill and the other in the refrigerator. Children can observe what happens over a period of a week or 10 days.

Activity 6: Do all plants need soil?

Give the children a range of containers and let them experiment with growing plants in different growing mediums, e.g. compost, soil, gravel, stones, sand, cotton wool, sawdust, water, without any growing medium at all. Do some plants grow better than others? Should we grow the same kind of plant in the different mediums to see which the plant grows best in?

Copymasters

Use copymaster 40 (What do plants need?) to show what conditions plants need to sustain life. Set up the conditions as shown on the sheet. The children can record their observations in the space alongside.

Area of study 2

WHAT ANIMALS NEED TO LIVE

C41

Purpose

To identify the conditions animals need to sustain life.

Materials needed

Collections of pictures and posters and wildlife videos, for example, David Attenborough's *Life on Earth*, different animals, animal homes or cages, a variety of animal foods, bird-table.

Activity 1

Watch the wildlife videos of as many different animals and their habitats as possible. If the language of the documentary is too difficult, turn the sound down and let the children make their own observations and comments. Talk about how suited the animals are to their environments and look at the animals' characteristics to see how they have adapted to their living conditions.

Activity 2

Take the pictures and sort them in different ways, for example, by type: mammals, birds, fish, insects, reptiles, amphibians; or by habitat: animals of the sea, forest, jungle, mountain, polar region and so on.

Activity 3

Talk about animals' needs. Animals need food and water. Look at the different foods that animals eat.

Some animals are herbivorous (eat only vegetation), some are carnivorous (eat only meat) and some are omnivorous (eat both vegetation and meat).

Look at animals' teeth. Compare plant eaters with meat eaters. How are their teeth different? Look at birds' beaks and feet. Look at animals' claws and hooves. See if the children can relate these adaptations to the animals' life styles. Look at the way animals move. How are land animals different from creatures that live in water?

Activity 4

Test different foods on different animals. Try and arrange for a selection of animals to come into school. First of all try them with various foods and observe their reaction; e.g. try cats with bird seed or a rabbit with a bone. Try to ascertain their favourite food from a selection of those which the owner says they will eat. Do remember that in strange conditions many animals will not eat at all.

Remember to conduct these tests carefully so as not to cause any distress to the animals and remember to consult DES and RSPCA regulations concerning keeping animals in school.

Activity 5

Set up the bird-table and supply a range of different foods such as seed, apple, bacon, nuts, and meat. Observe over a period of time and let the children record which foods are most popular with which species.

Favourite foods of our garden birds.					
Number of birds 7					
6					
5					
4					
3					
2					
1					
foods					

Activity 6

Try to find out about animals' homes and life styles. Look at their natural habitats and try to find pictures of their homes and the materials used to make them.

Activity 7

Try to find out how animals hunt for food. Do any use tools? (For example, the chimpanzee uses sticks to fish insects from holes.) Do any use traps like the spider which makes a web?

Activity 8

Categorise animals into those which live: alone; as a family group; in a herd or pack.

Copymasters

Use copymaster 41 (What do animals need?) to identify the needs of a chosen animal. Use the large box to draw or stick a picture of the animal on. Colour in the box with the name of the animal family or group, for example, if the animal is a shark then the child will draw a picture of one and colour the box with the word 'fish' in it.

The children then identify and colour the lifestyle symbol in the boxes below. By using a different sheet for each type of animal the children can build up a collection of the needs of different animal types.

CARING FOR LIVING THINGS

Area of study 3

C42

Purpose

To identify the sorts of things we need to do for the proper care and consideration of plants and animals.

Materials needed

Plant pots, fungicides, insect sprays, fertiliser, plant food, Leafshine, potting compost, scissors, collection of different plants.

Activity 1: Looking at plants

a) Look at photographs and pictures of healthy plants and animals and discuss with the children a set of criteria for good health. It will be useful here to have plant specimens which have strong stems and well-formed leaves without blemishes or infestations of pests or diseases. Talk about the remedies for helping a sick plant.

If the plant requires spraying for infestation or disease make sure the room is well ventilated or go outdoors. Do not let the children handle the sprays.

b) Look at some of the pests which attack plants, e.g. green or white fly or red spider mite, under the microscope or magnifying glass.

c) Examine the effects of a plant getting pot bound and let the children have a go at re-potting. Keep one plant of the same species in the small pot and observe which of the two plants grows best. Discuss with the children what they think might be the consequences of putting a plant into a pot which is too big.

Talk about care in handling plants, because the stems are easily broken. Show them how to take care in placing the roots in the pot to avoid damage.

d) Look at liquid manures such as Baby Bio. Set up a simple experiment with two plants of the same species and the same size. Feed one with the fertiliser and give the other just water. Compare results after a few weeks.

e) Try the plant product, Leafshine, on several types of plants and try to assess if the plant has benefited in any way.

f) Test for the effects of too much water, too little water, too much sun or not enough warmth.

g) See what happens if you pinch out the leaf tips over a period of time. Does the plant become bushier?

Perhaps different groups in the class could each have their own plant to care for over a few weeks and at the end of that time get together to decide whose plant looks the healthiest.

Activity 2: Look at animals

a) School animals or pets brought in from home can be used to work out a caring programme that the children can be involved in. (See copymaster 42.)

b) Try to arrange a visit to a local vet's surgery or ask the vet to come into school to talk to the children.

Make a veterinary surgery in a corner of the classroom using toy animals so that the children can reinforce what they have learned by role-play. Alternatively you could make a pet shop and bring in a range of pet care products. Discuss their suitability with the children.

Remember DES regulations about keeping animals in school and consult animal food manufacturers (Pedigree Petfoods have an extensive education section) and the RSPCA for advice on general petcare and safety.

Copymasters
Use copymaster 42 (Caring for pets) to record the number of times various care activities are to be done each week. Children draw their pet, or the school or visiting pet, and tick the boxes each time they complete a task.

Attainment target 3: Processes of life

Pupils should develop their knowledge and understanding of the organisation of living things and of the processes which characterise their survival and reproduction.

Level 2

Statements of attainment

Pupils should:

- know that living things reproduce their own kind.
- know that personal hygiene, food, exercise, rest and safety, and the proper and safe use of medicines are important.
- be able to give a simple account of the pattern of their own day.

Area of study 1

ALL LIVING THINGS REPRODUCE

C43

Purpose
To introduce the children to the idea that all living things reproduce their own kind.

Materials needed
Animals: pictures and photographs from magazines and books of a variety of animals and their young. (Try to find examples of the main orders, i.e. animals with backbones: mammals, birds, fish, reptiles, amphibians; animals without backbones: worms, jelly fish, sponges, insects, star fish and molluscs.)

Plants: seed catalogues and other pictures of a variety of plants from algae to trees, a selection of seeds of different sizes and types, a selection of plants from which to take cuttings, tubers and runners, a selection of bulbs and corms (if the time of year is appropriate), potting compost, pots, trays, appropriate garden tools, used lolly sticks or plastic drinking straws, card, glue, felt pens, Sellotape and scissors.

When introducing any animals into school, do make sure that they are safe to handle, non-toxic and housed and cared for at the highest standard. (See DES and RSPCA regulations and guidelines on keeping animals in school.) The same considerations on safety apply to plants.

Animals activity 1
(Due to the vast scope offered in this Attainment Target, it seems advisable to divide it into the plant and animal kingdoms and approach each as a separate small topic. In order to avoid confusions at this age and to cope with time restrictions, it would be best to choose from the range of activities listed below but to maintain variety.)

As a starting point try to bring in an animal which has just produced, or is about to produce, young. Avoid the larger mammals such as cats and dogs because the most 'reliable' animals can behave aggressively in defence of their young. Also remember that animals which produce litters of blind, unfurred young, such as rabbits, hamsters, and gerbils, often resort to eating the young when startled. However, guinea pigs, although rather shy animals, will tolerate careful handling of their young as they are born sighted, fully furred and able to eat solid food. They are good examples of young that resemble the adults from the moment of birth. Many other animals only later grow to look like the parents. Remember that most insect species have a larval and pupal stage before the young resemble adults.

Animals which offer few potential hazards, take up little space and do not need intensive care routines include stick insects, snails, worms, wood lice, frogs,

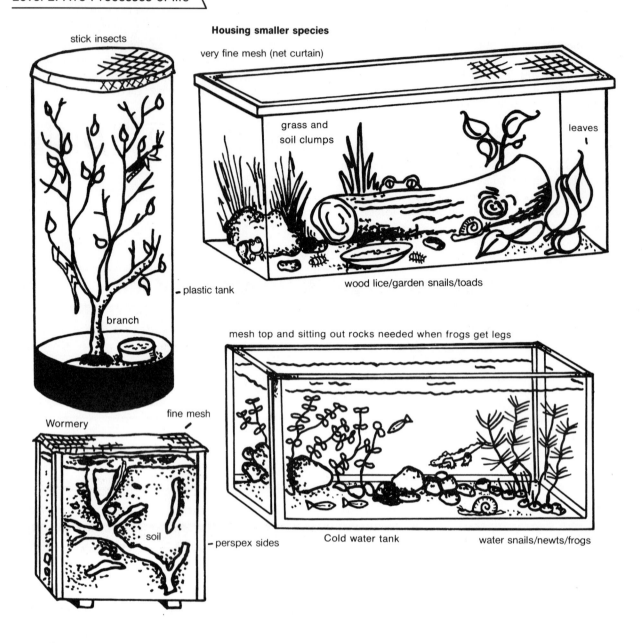

stick insects

Housing smaller species

very fine mesh (net curtain)

grass and soil clumps

leaves

plastic tank

branch

wood lice/garden snails/toads

Wormery

fine mesh

soil

perspex sides

mesh top and sitting out rocks needed when frogs get legs

Cold water tank

water snails/newts/frogs

toads and newts. For schools with a tropical fish tank, guppies are a common species, relatively easy to care for, which produce live young.

Incubation of chicken's or duck's eggs is difficult but potentially very rewarding as it is often possible for the children to witness hatching.

Animals activity 2
You may be able to visit a local farm which has young animals and caters for school parties. A good local zoo may have a pets' corner with animals such as goats, rabbits, fowl with their young.

One of the best examples of like producing like is the human being and it is usually possible to get one of the pupil's parents to bring in a young baby for the class to see.

If you can, let the children handle the animals and encourage them to observe differences and similarities between young and adult. Observe skin, fur, hair, eye development, limbs and mobility of young. Discuss dependence of young on the parent, what sort of food is taken by the young and how it is fed.

It will be wise to be fully conversant with the school's policy on sex education before embarking on the topic of reproduction, as it is necessary to be able to answer the children's questions as frankly as possible. Stimulated by the animal examples the children may ask many questions about 'how and why'. You will need to supply them with some information such as the fact that some animals give birth to live young and some lay eggs, unless of course you can provide actual examples or video material of the two types of birth. Methods of fertilisation vary from mating to the fertilisation of eggs which have been laid.

Animals activity 3
Animal families: you will need to teach the names and roles of the male, female and young in different animal families, for example, bull, cow, calf. To do this you can make a simple lotto game using pictures cut from magazines and old books. Players cover the base square with the other two family members and must also fill the whole grid or use up their cards.

Animals activity 4

Measure the weight of young animals as they grow and compare this with adult weight. Record findings on a graph.

Animals activity 5

Compare the gestation periods of different mammals or incubation periods of egg-laying species. Use a pictorial record (see below).

Animals activity 6

Compare numbers born to mothers in different species, e.g. one to six in humans, up to 10 in rabbits, a maximum of two in cows, and the vast numbers of eggs laid and hatched in species such as the frog and most insects.

Plants activity 1

As plants present far fewer problems and hazards in a classroom, collect a variety of plants to show different growth habits, colours, shapes and sizes. Try to provide plants which can be propagated in different ways, for example, runner, tuber, bulb, corm and cuttings (both stem and leaf).

Provide examples of different types of grass (in the flowering stage) and if you have trees near the school, provide a seed-bearing branch of a common species such as silver birch, scots pine or sycamore.

Discuss the similarities and differences between species and identify the reproductive parts of the plants, for example, the flowers, fruits, any formed seeds, runners, tubers, bulbs and corms. Encourage the children to identify differences and to enquire how and why these differences occur.

How long does it take for a baby to grow inside its mother?

	months																							
elephant	1	2	3	4	5	6	7	8	9	10	11	12	13	14	15	16	17	18	19	20	21	22	23	24
horse	1	2	3	4	5	6	7	8	9	10	11													
dog	1	2	(9 weeks)																					
cat	1	2	(8 weeks)																					
human	1	2	3	4	5	6	7	8	9	(40 weeks)														
mouse	1	(3 weeks)																						

For the sake of comparison, round off gestation times to whole months.

Plants activity 2

Measure the different parts of your plants for comparison. For example, obtain a sunflower head and a small flower head such as one of the separate umbels on a cow parsley and with more able children measure the area of both, using centimetre-squared paper. Both these plants are quite large but have different sized flowers and seeds. Make a collection of seeds: coconut, acorn, broad bean, nasturtium, cress, carrot and so on. Put them in order of size of seed and also (using pictures or examples of the plant) in the order of size of the plant. You can record your findings as a life sized picture and include a human to link the plant and animal kingdoms in their common biological purpose, i.e. reproduction (see below).

Many plants have runners which produce miniature plants, for example, strawberries, bramble or tradescantia. Measure the length of runners and count the number of runners on single plants.

Plants activity 3

Using your collection of seeds and pictures from seed catalogues, grow several kinds of plants (depending on time of year). Make labels using pictures stuck on to card and fixed to old lolly sticks.

Record the length of time for the seeds to germinate and then for the plant to flower. Encourage the children to notice similarities between the new plant and the picture of the parent plant. Save seeds from mature plants to re-plant. Obviously this is a long term project. If you can obtain a sunflower head to show the children, plant its seeds which will grow into a similar head.

Plants activity 4

Have a practical gardening session: take cuttings of stems from geraniums, busy Lizzie, etc.; take leaf cuttings from mother-in-law's-tongue or begonia; peg down runners on strawberries or tradescantia; plant bulbs, corms and tubers (try potato). Record different methods of propagation on zig-zag books.

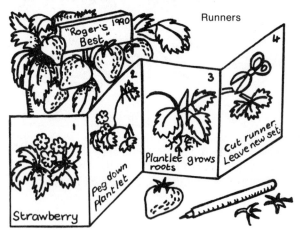

Copymasters

Use copymaster 43 (Can you match the families?) to record the composition of various animal families. There are four common farmyard families represented in the lists at the bottom of the sheet. The children refer to these to fill in the names of the animals on the pictures and then, using the colour code on the lists, they put the correct colour under the pictures to sort them into families.

GOOD HEALTH

C44

Purpose
To help children understand that taking care of personal health is important.

Materials needed
Large paper, felt pens, magazines, scissors, glue, photocopier or word processor, posters, videos, films, books on all aspects of good health.

Activity 1: Surveys
(There is tremendous scope in this part of Attainment Target 3. Indeed it could be said to outline an entire health education programme, the following activities will be useful to complement a long term topic on health.)

Show the children how to organise surveys on various topics in order to encourage them to question, to identify differences, list, collate and record information and later interpret their findings.

Surveys could be confined to the class or later include the rest of the school. Survey topics could include:

   Bedtimes in the class and/or getting up times
   Number of hours sleep each night
   Hobby activities which give exercise
   Hobby activities which are restful
   Eating habits (types of food eaten in a day)
   Most popular breakfast cereal
   Number of baths taken in a week
   Number of washes in a day
   Number of times teeth cleaned each day
   Most popular brand of toothpaste
   Number of parents who smoke
   Number of parents who have given up smoking
   Number of children who have been involved in a
      road accident
   Number of children who know the Green Cross Code.

In order to collect this material you will have to give the children some guidance on collection of inform-ation. In itself this could promote some useful discussion on how to approach people for questioning, what design to use for lists and charts, designing questions and most importantly interpreting results. It is essential that the survey is undertaken for a particular reason, for example, as a result of an unresolved question which arose in discussion or during a video on health. 'Do children like eating healthy food?' might be a typical question that arises in this way.

You will need to discuss the sort of questions children wish to put in surveys in order to ensure that they produce the right sort of information and are not ambiguous. You will also need to show the children various methods of duplication if they wish to produce several survey sheets.

name of child	Which of these foods did you eat yesterday?					
	fruit	meat	veg.	bread	cakes	sweets
Sue	✓	✓	✓			
Geoffrey	✓	✓	✓	✓	✓	✓
Michael	✓	✓	✓			
Anna		✓	✓	✓	✓	✓
Paul					✓	✓
Lizzie	✓	✓	✓	✓		
Steph	✓	✓	✓	✓		
Ian			✓	✓	✓	✓
Selina		✓	✓	✓		

Activity 2: Graphs and charts
Results of surveys can be recorded pictorially on large scale displays, for example:

Our favourite fruits

Activity 3: Visitors
Invite professionals into school to talk about their work. People such as the police, doctors, ambulance personnel, nurses and dentists are often willing to talk to children about their work as they feel it can help to improve health, prevent accidents and familiarise children with potentially frightening situations or people. The police will obviously have an input into the school on road safety and 'stranger danger'.

43

Activity 4: Role-play

This can be an invaluable learning situation even for the older child. Make a chemist's shop in a corner of the classroom which you can use for work on money and to reinforce learning on misuse of drugs and medicines. Similarly, make a food shop to promote healthy eating, or a doctor's surgery or hospital casualty department to reinforce learning about germs, accidents and safety. The visits from professionals will provide the children with stimulus, information and an example. Prepare questions before the visit for the children to ask them.

Activity 5: Posters and advertisements

After watching video material and finding out information from books, surveys, visitors and so on, get the children to design posters promoting all aspects of good health and warning about the pitfalls and dangers of neglect, e.g. danger when playing near pylons, railways or water, germs on unwashed hands, lack of exercise and heart disease. Find ways of reproducing some of the posters for distribution round school.

Activity 6: Make a newspaper

This could be for class or school distribution and can be devoted to health promotion. Articles can report on the results of your surveys. Think up 'shock horror' headlines such as 'Tooth decay eats its way through class!', 'Green fangs strike quiet classroom', 'Germ horror', etc. This paper could be the stimulus for the children to interpret their findings from the surveys. Include imaginative picture graphs of results and possibly some of the warning and promotional adverts.

A single copy wall newspaper could include photographs of things such as danger spots on local roads, railways and waterways as well as photos showing places for recreation. You could use a tape recorder to record some interviews with the visiting professionals or the actual transcript of the Green Cross Code. Make up mock interviews with self-confessed sweet addicts or mock interviews with sports idols.

Copymasters

Use copymaster 44 (Taking care of yourself) as one type of survey before designing your own with the children. Collate the findings on a graph or chart and interpret the results. The children may then think of something which needs doing as a result of this knowledge. Use the sheet with class members, teaching colleagues or the children's families, parents and siblings.

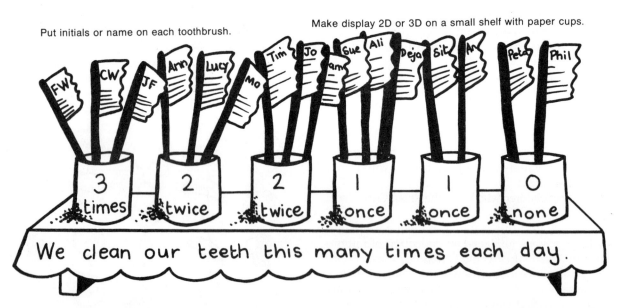

Put initials or name on each toothbrush.

Make display 2D or 3D on a small shelf with paper cups.

We clean our teeth this many times each day.

| Area of study 3 | **KEEPING A RECORD OF TIME** | C45 |

Purpose

To encourage the children to think sequentially about their own activities, and to record this methodically and accurately.

Materials needed

Drawing and writing materials, paper, tape recorder.

Activity 1

The types of surveys suggested in the second area of study will encourage the children to think about their own life styles, e.g. what exercise they take and when, what foods they eat, what times they go to bed and get up, when they have a bath and so on. This can easily lead to discussions about different life styles, cultural differences, routines on school days, holidays and weekends.

Activity 2
This can be done in conjunction with work on time. Introduce or revise the hour, half hour, quarter hour and so on.

Activity 3
Discuss the different getting up routines the children have. Include amusing episodes from everyone. 'How to get out of going to bed' could be the topic of a class discussion which you could tape record and play back later, both for enjoyment and to provide stimulus for further discussion on other parts of the day.

Activity 4
Go through the routine of your own weekday and possibly even commit it to a visual treatment, for example:

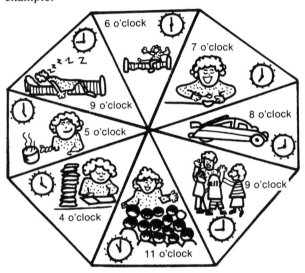

Discuss the routines which are fixed to certain days, e.g. 'Mum washes on Mondays and goes to Asda on Thursdays,' 'We have hymn practice on Thursday,' etc.

Discuss the spacing of activities and the possible reasons for this, for example, why we don't usually eat in the night, why we eat at the times we do in this country.

Activity 5
You could draw out a model day for a person who works at night, or draw a jumbled day, for example, breakfast, dinner, tea, bath, get up, go to sleep and so on.

Activity 6
When the children have had plenty of models and have some experience of times of the day, let them draw or describe their own typical school day, weekend day, holiday day. After discussing likes and dislikes in daily routines, they may enjoy designing an ideal day. The main point is to see that they understand the sequential nature of their own lives within the unchangeable order which nature imposes in terms of day and night, the need for food and rest, etc. Society also imposes an order on their lives.

Copymasters
Use copymaster 45 (My day) to record the different types of day the children experience. They can designate the day under the title, e.g., 'My day: Saturday', 'On holiday', 'Monday at school', etc. They are to draw in the time in the clock and draw the activity which they do at that time. This sheet can be enlarged to A3 for use on a wall display.

Attainment target 4: Genetics and evolution

Pupils should develop their knowledge and understanding of variation and its genetic and environmental causes and the basic mechanisms of inheritance, selection and evolution.

Level 2	**Statements of attainment**

Pupils should:

● be able to measure simple differences between each other.

 Area of study 1

OBSERVING DIFFERENCES C46

Purpose
To enable children to observe differences between each other.

Materials needed
Paint, ink, paper, scissors, black paper, anglepoise lamp, photographs of family members and the children themselves.

Activity 1
Talk about differences. Working as a class or in small groups get the children to talk about differences between each other, e.g. Do we all have the same colour hair or eyes? Are we all the same size?

Ask two children to stand side by side and ask the others to identify differences between them. Try to arrange for a mother and baby to come into school so that the children can make comparisons between themselves and the baby. Develop the language of comparison and discuss terms such as: longer/shorter, bigger/smaller, taller/shorter, wide/narrow. Look for differences in children's likes and dislikes.

Activity 2

Take a large sheet of paper and, laying it on the ground, draw round the smallest child in the group and then the biggest. The two outlines can then be painted in the likeness of the children and displayed side by side to show the differences in size at a glance.

Activity 3

Differences in clothes sizes can form the basis of ordering activities where the children can arrange a set of shirts in order from the largest to the smallest. They could sort from a collection of garments the clothes that they think will fit themselves. They can then try them on and decide whether the clothes fit well, are too small or too tight or too big. They can observe whether the tallest children always need the biggest shirt or the longest trousers or skirts. Ask them to see if clothes fit children in some places but not in others, for example, is the waist of a skirt too small but the length just right?

Activity 4

Children can take prints of hands and feet and place them in order of size. They can also look at the shape of both and compare other features such as fingerprints, lines on hands, shape of big toes, etc.

Activity 5

Encourage the children to look at the shape of faces. We all have differently shaped faces and the class could decide what shape each person has.

Look at the relationship between face shape and ethnic group and look at differences in features such as eye shape, noses, lips, ears and hair type.

round   oblong

square   triangular

Activity 6

Make a profile silhouette of a friend. Each child could make a silhouette portrait. Position an anglepoise lamp in a darkened room so that an accurate shadow of the child's profile is cast on a wall.

Pin a sheet of drawing paper to the wall and then the child can draw around the shadow. Some help may be needed to get the outline, after which the paper can be removed and the outline filled with black paint or felt pen. If preferred, paper which is white on one side and black on the other may be used, and after drawing on the white side the outline can then be cut out and reversed to give the black silhouette.

Remember to be aware of the dangers of misuse of electrical appliances. Some adult supervision is necessary for this activity.

Activity 7

Children can find out about family differences by drawing their own family tree, for example:

This will be useful for activities which require sorting for family size and for position in the family. A simple representation of this involves pre-cut-out shapes of father, mother, boy, girl, baby. These shapes can be cut out from highly coloured activity paper to make family group pictures.

Care must be taken to avoid prying into personal matters. Discussion will need to be of a sensitive nature bearing in mind, for example, one-parent families. Children can bring in photographs of themselves as babies and others in the class can try to identify them. This can promote a discussion about how much children have changed as they grow up.

Copymasters

Use copymaster 46 (All about me) to collect information about each child. The sheet can be taken home and the children may give as much information as they can or wish to. Parents may be enlisted to help with personal measurements such as height, weight, waist size and other facts and the information can be used as data for the work in Activity 2.

 Area of study 2

RECORDING AND INTERPRETING

 C47

Purpose

To record and interpret information about differences with the aid of charts and graphs.

Materials needed

Paper, pencils, crayons and coloured pencils, felt pens, scissors.

Activity 1

Using the information gathered in Area of Study 1 (pages 45–6) and also on copymaster 46 (All about me) devise charts and graphs as follows:

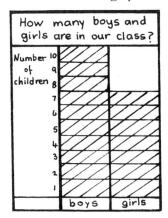

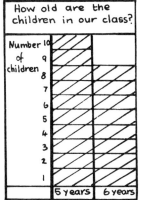

Activity 2

To record dental health or development draw a mouth map for each child and fill in teeth, gaps, cavities and permanent teeth. Draw two semi-circles and show 16 squares in each:

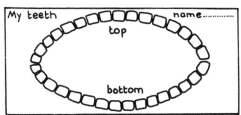

Choose different colours to represent the state of the teeth, for example:

healthy – white   fillings – blue
extractions – black   new teeth – red
cavities – brown

Activity 3

Other graphs could include shoe size, height, weight, hair colour, skin colour, children who wear glasses and so on. Discuss with the children the relationships within the class, for example, what is the commonest eye colour, skin colour, etc.

Copymasters

Use copymaster 47 (Elements of a graph). When compiling charts and graphs these symbols will save time. Children can colour in the pictures. The shoe symbol can be used to show different shoe sizes, the eye for eye colour, cake for birthdays, hand for skin colour and the face for hair type or race. Children can write their name in the shoe and this can be used in the graph below.

 Area of study 3

MEASURING DIFFERENCES

 C48

Purpose

To measure differences using standard and non-standard units of measurement.

Materials needed

Straws, strips of paper, matchboxes, rulers, tape measures, squared paper, trundle wheels, metre sticks, clocks, stop watches and timers, jug, bowl, water, sticky tape, large can, kitchen scales, seeds, sand, marbles.

Activity 1

Children can measure using non-standard units of measurement to begin with and rounding their own measurements to the nearest unit. Encourage them to measure different parts of the body.

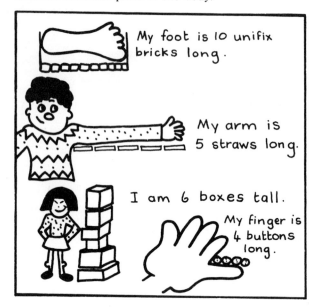

Stress the importance of starting the measurement at the beginning of the part to be measured and make sure the item is measured in a straight line to the end. Use different parts of the body to measure with.

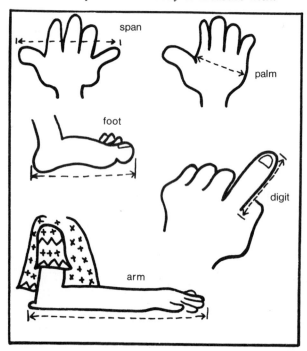

Discuss with the children whether measurements using different parts of the body are useful and reliable, e.g. compare a distance of five teacher hand spans with five child hand spans.

Activity 2

Discuss why it is important to have standard units of measurement such as centimetres and metres. Use strips of paper to measure the length of arms, legs, hands, feet, height and head size. These strips can be coloured and mounted in order of size.

Activity 3

Use squared paper to measure area of hand, foot and even body. On large areas colour in blocks of 10, using a range of colours, then count up in tens.

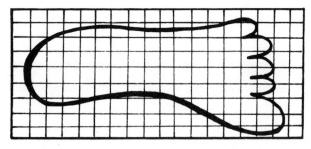

Activity 4

Children can use centimetre strips to measure actual height. Set up a 150 cm strip, marked off in centimetres. Children can work together to measure each other's height. Each child can then colour a centimetre strip of their own height (use two colours) and the collection can be mounted as a graph with flags sticking from the top of each strip for the child's name. Arrange strips in order of size or in class groups by gender. Alternatively, mark each child's height on the wall next to a long strip. Put the child's name next to the correct height.

Measure strides or arm span using centimetre strips, metre sticks or tape measures.

Activity 5

Use bathroom scales to measure children's weight. Most children can learn to read the weights shown but if not then the teacher can do so and children can record on a simple chart.

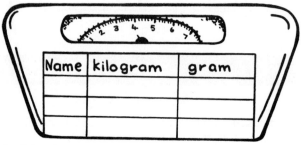

Activity 6

Discuss the findings with the children. Is the tallest child always the heaviest? Is the tallest child the one with the greatest stride or widest arm span?

Activity 7

Other measurements can include: Who can reach the highest? Who can jump up highest? (Children can try to make a chalk mark on the wall to mark their limit.) Who can jump farthest? (Make a start mark on the playground and with feet together do a standing jump forwards. Tape measures can be used to measure distances or for less able children use non-standard measurements.) Who can balance on one leg for the longest time? (Use clock or timer.) Whose hand is biggest? (Take a tall narrow jug, preferably plastic, half fill it with water and mark the water level. Children take it in turns to put one hand in the water up to the wrist and note how high the water rises.)

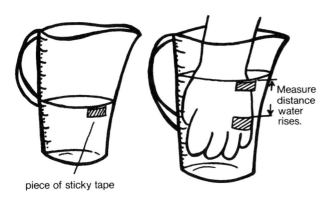

piece of sticky tape

Measure distance water rises.

Activity 8

Compare the left hand and the right hand and compare sizes with other children. Teacher can measure the rise and fall of the water. Remember to keep the water level topped up to the original level, since some water will be lost each time on children's hands.

A variation of this is to stand the jug in a bowl and fill it up to the brim. The amount of water displaced by each child can then be measured using a measuring jug or beaker. The children may need some help to do this.

Whose hand holds most? Measure how much each child can pick up. Take a large container and fill with marbles, beads, sand or sunflower seeds. Children can see how much they can pick up with their right hand. They can count the seeds and larger objects and weigh the sand.

Copymasters

Use copymaster 48 (I can do this) to record some of the measurements taken. Children can fill in their measurements in the spaces on the sheet.

Attainment target 5: Human influences on the Earth

Pupils should develop their knowledge and understanding of the ways in which human activities affect the Earth.

Level 2

Statements of attainment

Pupils should:

- know that some waste products decay naturally but often do so over a long period of time.
- be able to keep a diary, in a variety of forms, of change over time.

| Area of study 1 | **IDENTIFYING WASTE** | C49 |

Purpose

To identify which waste is made from natural substances, which from man-made substances, and which is a mixture of both.

Materials needed

Plastic bags, rubber gloves, tongs, waste samples.

Activity 1

As in Attainment Target 5, Level 1, discuss the kind of activities which produce waste of different types. Take a walk around school and collect as many examples of solid waste as is feasible from the point of view of safety and hygiene. Try to find examples of paper and plastic, metals (such as drinks cans and food cans), glass, food and garden waste. Some items will be made of both organic and inorganic materials, e.g. a food can will have a paper label (organic) on its metal (inorganic) body.

Do warn children against touching sharp edges of cans and broken glass and any substances which could be toxic, e.g. any sort of cleaning materials to be found in the caretaker's cupboard. Pressurised cans can also be dangerous and should not be punctured or incinerated. You could make a valuable topic from the starting point of danger in school. (See Attainment Target 3, page 5.) Children collecting waste should wear plastic gloves and wash their hands afterwards. Plastic tongs can also be used to handle waste in the classroom.

Activity 2
Back in the classroom, sort the waste according to type of materials: plastic, paper, wood, metal (aluminium, steel, iron, tin – these can be sorted into iron-based ones and non-iron-based by using a magnet), cloth, rubber, plants, animal waste and mixtures of materials such as glass and paper, and most foods. Label the different materials.

Activity 3
Looking at the materials collected, discuss the different origins of each. You will need to give the children some information, or the means of finding it

for themselves, e.g. books, addresses to write to (the Forestry Commission, the Coal Board, a glass manufacturer and so on).

You can now help the children to sort the materials into three sets:

1 Natural materials: a) organic: those which are of plant or animal origin and therefore were once alive; b) inorganic: those which occur naturally but were never alive, such as rocks and various metals
2 Man-made materials, such as plastics and some metals.
3 Mixtures of natural and man-made materials.

Copymasters
Use copymaster 49 (Rubbish collection) to record this activity. The children can draw items in the three categories or, where possible, stick on tiny samples. An A3 size sheet can be photocopied for use in class and larger and more awkward samples can be included for class display. Items which are liable to decay quickly, such as leaves, can be sandwiched between two layers of clear Contact® or Fablon®, which in some cases will preserve them for quite a time and in others at least isolate the material for viewing.

 TESTING FOR DECAY

Purpose
To show that some materials decay over a period of time.

Materials needed
Jam jars, card, pens, Sellotape, old spoons, waste samples.

Activity 1
Discuss what happens to waste material after it is left in the bin, goes down the plug hole and so on. You could also talk about recycling of different wastes. Take a walk round school or the local neighbourhood, looking out for decaying material of different kinds. Notice what conditions are present, e.g. whether it is wet, dry, cold, warm, open to the air, closed from the air, in the soil, in water and so on.

Activity 2
Set up a series of simple experiments to find out if waste material changes (decays) and if so, how long this takes and what happens to the material.
a) Use the solid wastes you collected in the first activity. You will need to discuss the need for a fair test and what conditions are needed in this case. Discuss the need to cut down the number of variables so that the factors you wish to test can be isolated, for example, get the children to see that if you use pieces of the same size and shape then each material has an equal chance of being affected by the decaying agent. Large pieces may take longer to

decay than smaller ones in the same material.

Decide on the size of the sample (make allowance for odd shaped items like apple cores, orange peel, sweets). Decide which conditions to use, for example, in the air indoors, in the air outdoors, in water, in soil, in sand, in peat, in compost. Decide on a period of time to leave the samples.

Label each sample with the name of the material and the date.

Make detailed observations of the materials over regular periods within your designated time and at the end of that time decide from your findings which materials have changed, how they have changed, how much decay has occurred, which have not been affected, which conditions were most favourable to decay in which materials. Do the test for each material then do it again for each but this time enclose the sample in a piece of sticky-backed plastic. This should slow down the process of decay. Use copymaster 50 to record this activity.

As plastics generally do not decay, discuss the significance of using plastic bin bags for refuse which is dumped in land-fill tips. Today many toys are made from plastics, but in past times materials such as fabrics and straw, tin and lead were used. The children may like to consider the significance of their own plastic toys never decaying.

b) Look at waste water around school. Collect samples of used hand washing water, used washing-up water, used clothes washing water, water used for washing paints, water used for washing glue pots. Discuss what makes water dirty and then what happens to waste water of various types. Observe what happens if the water is left to settle for a period of time, which is part of the water purification process used by water treatment plants.

Put each type of water in a jam jar, with a cover on the top and label with the date and leave it for a period. Start with a week and continue for further weeks if you wish to continue the observation for any reason. Simply observe the condition of the water at the start of the time and at regular intervals. The heavier contents of the water, for example, bits of food, powder paints, etc. will fall to the bottom of the jar and the water higher in the jar will become clearer. Some of the solid contents will produce gases as they decay, so lift the lids carefully and smell the air given off. Record observations pictorially.

c) You could test the purity of your separated water on plants. For a short time, water one with 'clean' tap water, one with the dirtiest water from your collection and one with separated water. See which one seems to suit your plants the best. Discuss how to make this a fair test.

d) Decaying material produces gases. To show this, set up an experiment, putting waste products in large, clear bottles and placing a deflated balloon over the top of each bottle. Observe the balloons, which will begin to inflate as the decaying material gives off gases. Include a 'control' to show the children that if there is no decaying material then no gas is produced. Record the length of time it took for the balloon to become erect, or at least slightly erect.

Does waste make gas?			
waste	day 1	day 2	day 3
no waste			
food			
soil and water		*Use same size clear bottles. Pull mouth of balloon over neck of bottle. Add date.*	
paper and plastic			

Copymasters

Use copymaster 50 (What rots?) to record the investigation on solid wastes. A small sample of the material can be stuck on the sheet if practical. The children can record observations weekly by drawing what the sample looks like. Use a separate sheet for each material tested.

DIARIES

Purpose

To show that changes over time can be recorded. (Recording change over time is an integral part of most investigations as change itself is part of life. Children need to become accustomed to recording a variety of events sequentially and accurately and using time as part of this process.)

Materials needed

Paper, card, felt pens, camera, tape recorder.

Activity 1: Make a class timetable, like a comic strip

Either cut out pictures from magazines or get the children to draw the activities. Include the time of each activity in the form of a clock and words. Ask the children to try to remember which activities are done on which day. The children may like to make up their own 'ideal' timetable! (See illustration below.)

Activity 2: Make a record of personal growth

Ask the children to bring in photographs of themselves at various ages. They could also bring in photos of other relatives. Put these into a sequence of development using a zig-zag book as a base. Write the age of the child and the date (year) next to each photo.

Activity 3: Photograph events

If there is any building going on in the neighbourhood of school, make a photographic record of the progress from foundations and up to the roof. Include a child in the photograph holding a large board showing the date. Display the photographs in sequence on a zig-zag book or as a wall, the photos mounted on bricks.

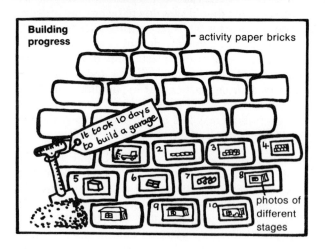

Building progress — activity paper bricks

It took 10 days to build a garage

photos of different stages

Activity 4: Make a growing book

To record the growth of linear things like plants, measure the exact growth each week or more often and draw the plant to that height on equally wide pieces of paper. Staple together as a book which will look like the finished plant. Note the date on each leaf of the book.

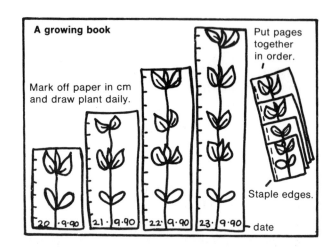

A growing book

Put pages together in order.

Mark off paper in cm and draw plant daily.

20·9·90   21·9·90   22·9·90   23·9·90 — date

Staple edges.

Monday
writing and number
Playtime
painting
Lunch time
games
Playtime
story
Cinderella
Little Toot
Pen Pete
Home time

Activity 5: Keep a sound archive

Record an event as it happens, using a tape recorder. Choose an event such as sports day where there are several things going on over a period of time and the reporter can update the time constantly. Alternatively record daily progress on a project, for example, a conservation project, with a 9 o'clock bulletin from the site: 'It's Tuesday 25 March and here we are by the pond. Work has been going on for four days now and we are at last . . .'

Activity 6: Make a birthday board

As part of your normal class routine make a record of children's birthdays as they occur. Note day, month, year and age.

Activity 7: Keep a comic strip record

Record daily changes of events such as the weather, using a linear strip to which further weeks can be added if you wish. Note day and date.

Activity 8: Circular events

The yearly pattern of the seasons can be charted on a circular picture. As the seasons blend into each other, no definite linear division is needed. Use cut-out pictures drawn by the children showing their activities, e.g. snowballing, and use cut-outs from garden magazines to give a montage picture of plants and weather and human activity. Fill in the chart as the year progresses.

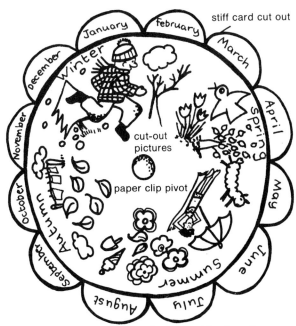

stiff card cut out

cut-out pictures

paper clip pivot

Use a different colour for the backing board.

Copymasters

Use copymaster 51 (Diary) to record a sequence of events. Children can put in the date and time if necessary.

☁ ☂ ☀ January 1991 ☀ ☂ ☁						
Monday	Tuesday	Wednesday	Thursday	Friday	Saturday	Sunday
7th.	8th.	9th.	10th.	11th.	12th.	13th.
Monday	Tuesday	Wednesday	Thursday	Friday	Saturday	Sunday
14th.	15th.	16th.	17th.	18th.	19th.	20th.

Attainment target 6: Types and uses of materials

Pupils should develop their knowledge and understanding of the properties of materials and the way properties of materials determine their uses and form the basis for their classification.

Level 2

Statements of attainment

Pupils should:

- be able to recognise important similarities and differences, including hardness, flexibility and transparency, in the characteristics of materials.
- be able to group materials according to their characteristics.
- know that heating and cooling materials can cause them to melt or solidify or change permanently.

Area of study 1

IDENTIFYING MATERIALS
C52

Purpose
To enable children to identify the main characteristics of different materials.

Materials needed
Range of materials including: wood (from balsa through to hardwoods), paper (from tissue through to thick card, corrugated card, tracing paper, wallpaper), rubber (from rubber bands to inner tubes), plastics (from fine plastic bags to heavy duty, rigid and corrugated plastic), metals (including lead, aluminium, iron, steel, tin foil, brass, copper, zinc), stone (including chalk, limestone, granite, sandstone), coal, brick, concrete and other mixtures of manufactured materials, glass (from sheet glass – clear, translucent, opaque, toughened – to glass cobblestones and glass waste), ceramics (from eggshell china to heavy earthenware).

Activity 1
Display all the materials together and give the children as much opportunity as possible to handle and talk about them.

Activity 2
Ask the children if they can think of any words to describe the materials. They will probably come up with straightforward descriptive words such as hard, heavy, soft, bendy, stiff and so on. Begin with the words on copymaster 52 (Looking at materials), relate the words the children use to the list shown and explain the ones they are not familiar with. Then group the words into opposites, for example, hard/soft, rough/smooth, dull/shiny, heavy/light, hard/malleable, rigid/flexible, bounces/does not, absorbent/waterproof, stretches/tears, transparent, translucent/opaque.

Activity 3
Taking just two sets of characteristics, the children can sort the materials and make two separate sets, e.g. these things are hard/these things are soft. This activity will promote a lot of discussion and will encourage the children to make their own value judgements, initially involving their senses.

Copymasters
Use copymaster 52 (Looking at materials) to identify the characteristics of the range of materials listed. Children take the material and tick the appropriate boxes on the chart according to the characteristics they observe.

Area of study 2

CLASSIFYING MATERIALS
C53

Purpose
To identify materials which have similar characteristics and to group them together.

Materials needed
Clay, stones, shoe boxes, blocks of wood or plastic Lego®/building blocks, PVA glue, scissors, card, paint, paper, Sellotape, Cellophane, clear plastic sheeting, plastic film, corrugated plastic sheet, hand saw.

Activity 1
Arrange a visit to a building site to enable the children to observe the variety of materials in use and to look at the way the materials are used and how they are joined together.

Remember that building sites are potentially dangerous places so do not let the children get too close to any of the constructional activity. Stand a safe distance away and if possible ask for small samples of the materials used.

Activity 2

If such a visit is not possible or not advisable, take a walk around the school and try to identify the materials used in its construction. Look at walls, doors, windows, partitions, floors, ceilings and so on. It might even be possible, provided there is easy access, to go into the loft space and look at the joists and roof supports.

Activity 3

To follow up this observation set the children the task of building their own play house using scrap material. Discussion and planning will be an important part of this activity. They will need to think about overall dimensions, what materials they are going to use and major constructional problems such as how to support the roof and how to hang the door.

If the materials they have seen used in construction of a real building are not suitable for their purpose, then this will result in the search for a suitable alternative: materials which will do the same task and which might have the same or similar characteristics. For example, when the children have decided on the size of the house, they will need to choose a suitable material for the walls. This might be shoe boxes, blocks of wood, Lego®, thick card sheets or whatever they think is most suitable, subject to availability.

The working of different materials and the tools needed are another important consideration. Cutting glass would be difficult and inadvisable in the school situation, therefore an alternative material would be needed which could do the same job and be easy to handle. The children might choose from a range of alternatives such as perspex, rigid plastic, clear plastic film, Cellophane or Coverlon®.

These same considerations will apply to the rest of the house and much experimenting can be done to test the appropriateness of the alternative materials, for example, if the roof needs to be waterproof (and you may decide it does not if the house is sited indoors) then the children can experiment with various materials which may be suitable such as PVA glue, wax, plastic sheeting. Test by pouring water over it.

This could raise questions about design, such as 'Is a flat roof better than a sloping one?'

Copymasters

Use copymaster 53 (Grouping materials) to identify materials which have the same or similar characteristics. Using the practical experience they have gained from the activities and also the checklist on copymaster 52, the children are to choose three different materials which have similar characteristics and group them together in the spaces provided next to the structure for which they could be used, i.e. roof, window, door and wall.

 CHANGES

Area of study 3

C54

Purpose

To show that heating and cooling materials can cause them to melt or solidify or change permanently.

Materials needed

Candles, wax crayons, water, pan, heat source, ice, fridge, bottle, clay, kiln, lolly sticks, paper, fabric, eggs, balloons, recipe and ingredients; iron, bottle and plastic bag, saucer, bucket, Plasticine®, coloured inks.

All experiments involving heat should be supervised by an adult.

Activity 1

Look at the effect of heat and cold on a range of different materials.

One of the easiest materials to use when studying the effect of heat is wax. Examine some wax in its cold state and identify its characteristics, for example, when cold it is brittle, hard, greasy and solid; when warmed in the hand it becomes softer and more malleable but is still solid; when heated to a high temperature it changes its state and becomes a liquid. To return it to the solid state, carefully drop a small quantity into a bucket of cold water. You will notice that the wax floats on the surface. An interesting way of reinforcing this fact is to do some batik.

Activity 2: Batik

The wax is put in a pan and heated and the children can see it change from a solid to a liquid. In this state it can be painted, trailed or dripped to make a design on fabric. When the wax has hardened the material is crumpled to produce cracks in the wax. The material is then soaked in cold water dye and when the desired colours are achieved, it is taken out and dried. The material is then ironed between sheets of brown paper or newspaper, which soaks up the melting wax. A very pleasing effect is achieved as a result of the dye soaking into the cracks and the rest of the wax acting as a barrier to show the outline of the design in the original colour of the material where the dye could not reach.

Activity 3: Reflections

Draw a design on paper using heavily applied wax crayon. Put another sheet of paper on top and iron this with a hot iron. As the wax melts, the design is transferred on to the new sheet.

Activity 4: Ice/water/steam

Temperature changes water. Show this to the children by melting ice cubes in a pan. You can then re-freeze the water or continue boiling it until all the water has turned to steam. Hold a cold plate well above the steam and watch it condense again into water.

Ice cubes can be used to keep the plate cold.

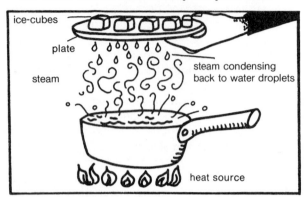

Activity 5: Heat changes food

The effect of heat on food can be interesting and delicious. A simple observation would be to look at the difference between a raw egg and others which have been boiled for one minute, three and seven minutes respectively.

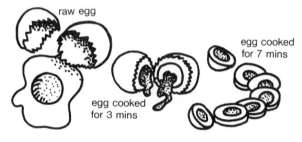

Activity 6: Make a cake

Mix the ingredients for a cake, then keep a little of the mixture to one side and bake the rest. When the cake is cooked, the children will be able to observe differences of texture, taste, smell, colour and so on between the two. They will also like to taste the end product.

Activity 7: Cook vegetables

Try eating a variety of vegetables and noting texture, smell, taste and colour, then cook them and compare the same features after cooking. Children can experiment to find out cooking times for different foods.

Activity 8: Throw some clay

Clay is another material which changes when heat is applied. The children can be given a piece of clay and asked what they can do to it or with it. Ask the children to try pulling, pinching, stretching, rolling, flattening and squashing it. They can then bake their effort in an oven or kiln or put it on top of a radiator or in a warm place and observe how it dries out, how long this takes in each case and finally how hard the resulting pot is, depending on the drying method.

Activity 9: Enamelling

If there is a kiln in school, glass can be melted and very interesting effects produced by enamelling on copper.

Activity 10: Crack a bottle

Fill a glass bottle to the brim with water and screw the lid on tightly. Put this in the freezer compartment of a fridge overnight. As the water expands when it freezes, it should at least crack the bottle.

To protect against broken glass, put the bottle in a plastic bag.

Activity 11: Wax wonder

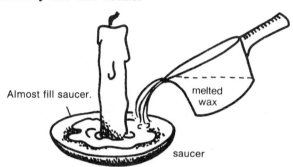

Melt a candle in a pan along with a brightly coloured pure wax crayon. Stick another candle to a saucer, using a little of the melted wax. Pour the rest of the melted wax on to the saucer around the base of the candle.

Next, fill a bucket with water. Hold the candle at the top and taking care not to spill the molten wax, plunge the candle on its saucer straight down into the water. Make sure the candle is vertical and as you plunge, twist the candle and saucer around.

The molten wax will want to rise to the surface but the cold water will make it solidify before it reaches its goal and will set the wax in the most unusual swirling shapes.

This activity is for an adult. Wear rubber gloves as sometimes the wax rises upward to the hand before it has cooled sufficiently.

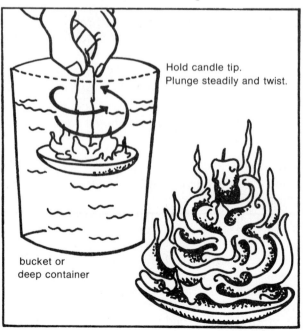

These fantasy candles can be lit and the shapes of the wax produce fascinating shadows, glows and gleams. The candles can look like many things, from castles to strange creatures, and could provide much stimulus for creative writing.

Activity 12
Model with Plasticine®. When cold it is hard and difficult to work, but even the heat of the hand can make it more pliable and manageable.

Activity 13: Ice balloons
To make an ice balloon simply fill a balloon with water, tie the neck and put it in the freezer compartment of the fridge. When frozen solid, cut the neck of the balloon and peel away the rest leaving an ovoid of ice. If coloured inks are included when the water is first poured in, the resulting colours will produce an interesting effect in the balloons.

The ice balloons can be floated in water for the children to look at.

Activity 14: Permanent change
Some materials can be changed permanently especially if they are burnt: for example, paper and wood (e.g. lolly sticks) change to ash and charcoal. If you are going to demonstrate this in school do remember safety considerations.

Copymasters
Use copymaster 54 (Changes) to record the effects of heating and cooling on the materials shown. The children can draw a picture from direct observation in the space provided.

Attainment target 9: Earth and atmosphere

Pupils should develop their knowledge and understanding of the structure and main features of the Earth, the atmosphere and their changes over time.

Level 2

Statements of attainment
Pupils should:

- know that there are patterns in the weather which are related to seasonal changes.
- know that the weather has a powerful effect on people's lives.
- be able to record the weather over a period of time, in words, drawings and charts or other forms of communication.
- be able to sort natural materials into broad groups according to observable features.

 WEATHER AND THE SEASONS

Area of study 1

Purpose
To show that weather and the seasons have a powerful effect on our lives.

Materials needed
Video material of weather (different types of weather around the world, weather forecasts, news items about fantastic weather conditions, sports and pastimes relating to different seasons and weather conditions such as skiing), pictures of different types of weather, clothes for different seasons and hobbies, a world globe, metal or plastic piping and various fabrics, barley, wheat, small containers, compost, paper and paints.

Activity 1
Introduce the topic with a dramatic video sequence such as a downhill ski run or news coverage of a

hurricane. Talk about the weather shown on the video and compare it with the weather in your area today. Ask questions such as: Is it cold or is it hot? Is it wet or is it dry? Is it sunny or is it dull? Is it windy or still? Do you like the weather today? Do you think the weather will change today? What was the weather like yesterday? What do you think it will be like tomorrow?

Look at the collection of pictures and ask the same questions. Make the point that these conditions change daily and are what we call weather. This varies according to the season.

Activity 2
Revise the seasons. Think up pictorial symbols for different types of weather.

The children will enjoy reminiscing about 'weather I have known': the time rain washed away a garden,

sunny

dull with sunny spells

rain

wind

Activity 5

Talk about the effects of temperature on our bodies, particularly on the very old and the very young. Discuss the effects of extreme cold on our homes. We need to use heating appliances and sometimes pipes freeze. To illustrate this get some strips of metal or plastic piping and blocking one end with Plasticine® fill these with water to represent household water pipes. Put one in the freezer (if you have access to one),

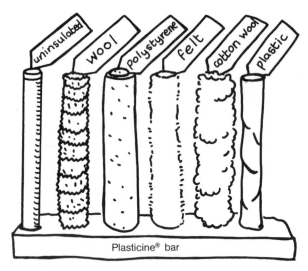

Plasticine® bar

uninsulated, and think of several different materials with which to insulate the rest, such as metal foil, polystyrene, wool, felt, cardboard, newspaper, plastic sheeting. These should also go into the freezer and the effect of the insulation noted. Keep one as a control, representing a pipe which is indoors, or not in freezing conditions.

when the wind blew the washing into next door's garden, when it was so hot they had tea in the paddling pool and so on. Sort the symbols into sets of weather associated with the four seasons. Paint pictures of the major seasonal types of weather.

Activity 3: Temperature

Talk about the association between temperature and seasons, e.g. sunny and cold in the winter or sunny and warm in the summer. Think of as many different temperature words as possible, such as warm, cool, hot, cold, freezing, sweltering.

Take the temperature in the classroom and outside in the playground over a period of a week and record it on a weather chart. (See the next Area of Study.) Let the children decide individually what they think the day feels like and record this subjective assessment also.

Activity 6

You can also discuss the types of food we eat in different seasons and why this may be so, related to the temperature.

Activity 7

Show video material of different parts of the world (wildlife videos are useful for this purpose) and talk about the obvious signs of temperature differences

Activity 4

To illustrate the effects of temperature on the crops we grow for food, grow some barley or wheat in small containers and expose one batch of seedlings to the effect of frost by placing it in the coldest part of a fridge for the night, so that some ice forms on it. Expose another batch to extreme heat near a radiator or in a cool oven and leave one batch as a control in a cool place in school. Observe and note what happens to each.

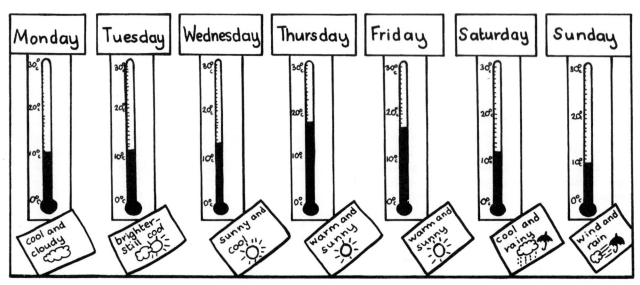

such as snow, scorched grass, high windy mountains, jungles, people wearing different types of clothes. Using a globe, show the children where the equator and the poles are and, using a large beach ball as the Sun, try to illustrate how the equator is nearer the Sun and therefore warmer.

Activity 8: Look at clouds

Collect pictures of clouds, either by photo or cut out from magazines or old books. Some children will be able to learn the names, but it is more important that they try to identify which clouds give rain showers, which give steady rain and which never give rain. Whilst warning of the danger of looking directly at the sun, spend some time cloud watching. Look at the way clouds change shape and how fast they go and in what direction they move. Are there any clouds which are man-made, such as jet trails, smoke from industrial chimneys or cooling towers?

Activity 9: Rain

Talk about the effect rain has on our lives. You may be able to get hold of news features of floods showing crops and homes damaged by rainstorms, or drought conditions with people queueing for water at stand-pipes, dry reservoirs or extreme Third World conditions where the long term effect of drought causes famine.

Look at rain washing down a window pane; watch it drop onto blotting paper or kitchen towel and look at the size of the blobs.

Activity 10

Make a rain gauge. (See the next Area of Study.)

Activity 11: Look at wind

Go outside and feel it. Make a wind using large sheets of thick card. Make flags using cloth and rolled paper sticks and watch them blow in the wind. You can also make card windmills and simple kites.

Activity 11: Look at wind direction

Make a weather vane. (See the next Area of Study.) Ask the children to try and think of ways of finding the wind direction. Ask questions such as: Do the clouds move? What do you think is moving them? Are they all moving at the same speed? Are they all moving in the same direction?

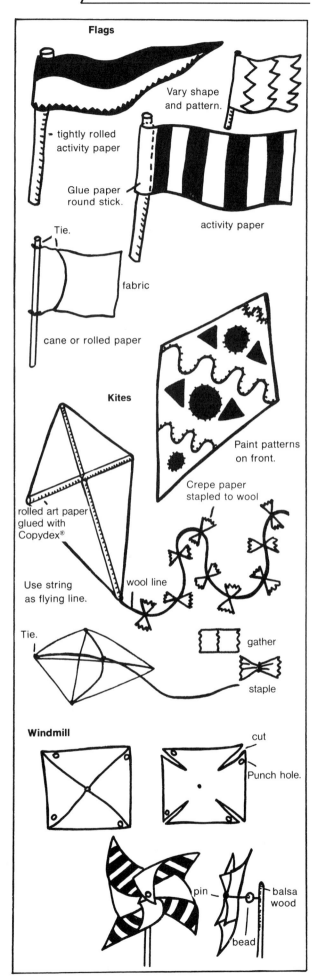

59

Activity 12

Does the wind move at the same speed and in the same direction nearer the ground? Watch a weather vane, a wind sock, washing on a line, litter on the ground, the grass, crops in a field. Hold up a wet finger to feel which way the wind is blowing.

How strong is the wind? Look at the Beaufort Scale and see if you can guess the speed of the wind today.

The Beaufort Scale		
Description and wind speed	Effect	Force
Calm 0 m.p.h.		0
light breeze 2-5 m.p.h.		1-2
moderate breeze 10-15 m.p.h.		3-4
strong breeze 20-30 m.p.h.		5-6
moderate gale 35-45 m.p.h.		7-8
gale 50-60 m.p.h.		9-10
storm/hurricane 70 m.p.h. and above		11-12

Activity 13: Does the wind affect the temperature?

Tell Aesop's fable of the Sun and the Wind who each try to persuade a traveller to remove his coat.

Activity 14

Talk about the type of clothes needed for each season and make a collection of clothes and aids such as sunglasses, umbrellas, sun visors. Display these with the different seasonal weather pictures.

Ask questions such as: Are your clothes right for today's weather? What do you wear at school when it is hot? What do you wear at home when it is hot? What do you like to wear in the rain? What do you like to wear in the snow? What do you wear on a windy day? What will you wear if the weather changes today? When do you get new clothes?

Activity 15: Sports

Talk about the sports which are played during the different seasons. Ask the children to bring in photographs of themselves engaged in any sporting activity or pastime such as tobogganing, swimming outdoors, horse riding, sailing. Discuss the type of clothes that are worn for sports. Talk about winter and summer sports and those which are played in all weathers. Some sports need special conditions such as wind for sailing, hang-gliding and windsurfing. Talk about the changes in the weather which might cause these sports to be cancelled, such as rain in the tennis season.

Copymasters

Use copymaster 55 (The seasons clock) to record some small part of the effect the weather has on our lives. The children can colour in the central motif, fill in the names of the seasons and draw the sort of clothes that they would wear at the different times.

Area of study 2	**RECORDING THE WEATHER**	C56

Purpose

To enable the children to record the weather over a period of time and in various forms.

Materials needed

An assortment of containers of different shapes (for example, yoghurt pot, milk bottle, glass, tin tray) paper, pens, rulers, scissors, glue, Sellotape, pine cones, an assortment of different types of wood in thin sheets about 30 cm square, string, a brush handle, paper plates, dowelling, drawing pins, saucers, a pair of tights, large clear plastic drinks bottle, seven small bottles to fit inside the latter.

Activity 1

Make a weather diary. Make a small notebook which can be filled in each day, or using copymaster 56 make a weekly chart to view a week's weather at a glance. The children can decide on appropriate symbols to use.

Activity 2

Record the temperature, using a simple Celsius thermometer or a dual one. Decide whether to take the temperature outdoors in an exposed or a sheltered place, or both. Record on a bar chart.

Activity 3: Record how much rain falls

Place an assortment of containers outside on a rainy day in an exposed spot. See which collected the most rain, which was the first to overflow and in which the water was deepest. Try to get the children to see that a standard measuring container is needed, whatever the shape.

A rain gauge can be made from a large, clear plastic drinks container, with the top cut off to make a funnel. Choose seven smaller bottles that will take the opening of your funnel and label these with the days of the week.

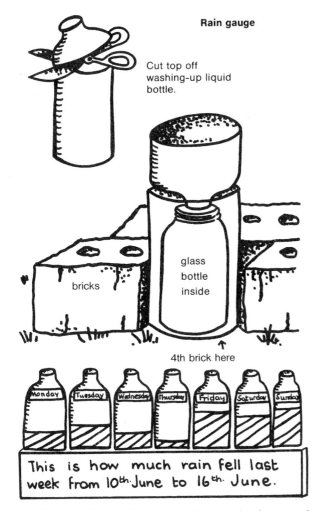

Rain gauge

Cut top off washing-up liquid bottle.

glass bottle inside

bricks

4th brick here

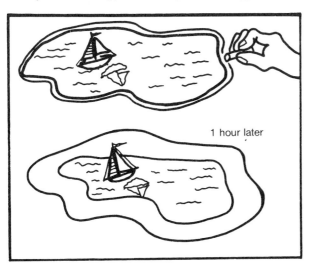

This is how much rain fell last week from 10th June to 16th June.

A display of the bottles themselves can be the record of a week's rainfall. Cover the tops of the bottles so that rain collected does not evaporate. As a result of the rainfall survey ask questions such as: When did the most rain fall? When did the least fall? On which days was there no rain? How many days of rainfall have there been this week?

Activity 4: Where does rain go to?

Measure puddles in the playground to watch the water evaporating. Simply chalk round the edge when the rain has stopped and at regular intervals, possibly hourly or half daily, until the puddle disappears.

Ask questions: What is the weather like now? Is it windy? Is it sunny? Why is the puddle smaller? Where has the water gone?

To prove the point about the contribution of the wind and the sun to evaporation, set up a small experiment with saucers of water. Put one saucerful on top of a radiator shelf or a windowsill near a radiator which is fully on. Mark the decrease of the water during the day or the week. Put a saucer of water in a cool place out of a draught, to act as a control. Put another saucerful in front of a major draught such as an open window and mark the decrease of the water here too.

Talk about washing drying in the wind and test how quickly several different types of material will dry, from thin nylon to heavy woollen cloth.

Activity 5

Look at the wind direction and its strength and try to relate this to observable effects such as if the wind is in a certain direction we get rain, if it is very strong the washing dries quicker than if it is less strong.

To find the wind direction make a simple wind sock using an old pair of tights and a piece of dowelling or a brush handle. Use a compass to show the children the direction.

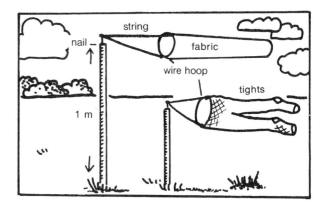

string
nail
fabric
wire hoop
tights
1 m

Put the wind sock in an exposed place. Record the activity on tape recorder to give practice in speaking and reportive work. You could also make a weather vane using wood. Find north and fix the vane in position.

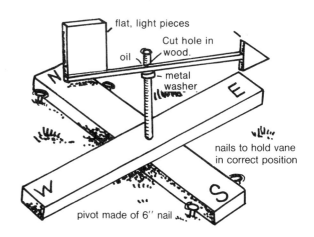

flat, light pieces
Cut hole in wood.
oil
metal washer
nails to hold vane in correct position
pivot made of 6" nail

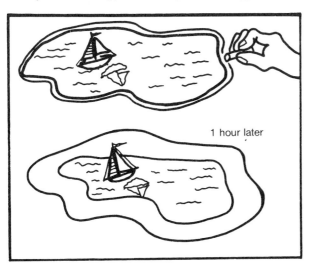

1 hour later

61

To make your own test of wind strength make a wooden washing line. Take a broom handle and fix to it, as shown, six squares of materials of different weight: tissue paper, thin card, thick card, thin wood, thick wood, a metal bar. Label these one to six. Hold this washing line out in the wind in different parts of the school grounds and record the wind strength. If the sheets up to number three move, then the wind strength is recorded as three.

Activity 6
Recording any of this work can be done in writing in a weather diary, or as speech on to a tape recorder. A simple and effective way of recording the week's weather would be to get two children each day to paint a picture of the weather morning and afternoon for a week. Label these with the day and date and display as a large frieze.

Copymasters
Use copymaster 56 (Weather record) to record weather over one week.

children's own paintings cut out

The weather this week in June 1990

| Monday | Tuesday | Wednesday | Thursday | Friday |

— children's paintings

NATURAL MATERIALS

Area of study 3

C57

Purpose
To help children sort and classify natural materials.

Materials needed
A wide range of different materials and objects in the categories of animal, vegetable and mineral. You can include one or two live things, bearing in mind the regulations about keeping animals in school.

Activity 1
Let the children handle and discuss a wide range of objects. Sort the objects for one category at a time. Tell the children that all things on earth are either animal, vegetable or mineral. Animals and vegetable things are alive or were once alive but minerals have never been alive. Some information will need to be received information because many objects will be of animal or vegetable origin, for example, a sheepskin rug, a woollen jumper, a basket, a piece of wood. Once the origin has been identified the children will probably be able to attempt classification. This will promote a lot of discussion, as it is a very difficult concept indeed and in fact the value of such an exercise is in this discussion as a result of direct observation.

Activity 2

Sort your objects for one category at a time, bearing in mind these broad characteristics:

Animal	*Vegetable*	*Mineral*
alive/ once alive	alive/ once alive	not alive/ never has been
moves	moves a little	doesn't move
breathes	breathes	doesn't breathe
destroyed if broken up	destroyed if broken up	not destroyed if broken up
makes a noise we hear	does not make a noise we hear	does not make a noise
has a smell	has a smell	has no smell
coloured	coloured	coloured
soft and hard	soft and hard	hard
variety of shapes (usually head, body, limbs)	variety of shapes (usually leaves, stems)	looks like rock

Copymasters

Use copymaster 57 (What is it?) to consolidate the discussion. Get the children to help you collect the items on the copymaster, and working together they can sort them into sets. Then they can draw them in sets on the sheet.

Attainment target 10: Forces

Pupils should develop their knowledge and understanding of forces; their nature, significance and effects on the movement of objects.

Level 2	**Statements of attainment**

Pupils should:

● understand that pushes and pulls can make things start moving, speed up, swerve or stop.

 Area of study 1 — # PUSHING AND PULLING C58

Purpose

To show the difference between pushing and pulling.

Materials needed

Pictures of things being pushed and pulled along, a brush, rope, ball, box, mat, bathroom scales, spring balance.

Activity 1

Collect as many pictures as possible which show different things being pushed and pulled, e.g. a train pulling carriages, a car pulling a caravan and a large truck pulling a trailer. Show these alongside pictures of things being pushed, like a sailing boat pushed along by the wind, a kite in the air, a wheelbarrow and a brush being used to sweep up leaves, etc. A small display can be made using children's toys to show pushing and pulling and the children can handle these in order to test for what is needed in order to make the object move. The objects can then be sorted into two groups: those that need to be pushed along and those that need to be pulled.

Activity 2

Sometimes we need to both push and pull when doing a particular thing. Discuss with the children a variety of different actions which might involve both pushing and pulling such as writing, sweeping the floor, riding a bicycle, a tug of war, rolling a ball, climbing a rope or a ladder. Let the children try to do each of the activities and they can discuss whether they need to push or pull and which parts of the body are needed to do this.

They will find out that some activities involve both, e.g. pulling with arms one way and pushing against the floor with legs in the opposite direction as in a tug of war. By trying the activities for themselves the children should hopefully come to the conclusion that pulling involves drawing things towards themselves while pushing involves moving things away.

Activity 3

To test the strength of their push children can set up a pair of bathroom scales against the wall, making sure they are at the correct height for the child to be able to push well. As each child pushes against the scales, the teacher can record the reading.

Activity 4

To test the strength of pull, the children can pull on a heavy duty spring balance either held by the teacher or securely fixed to a wall. As before the teacher can read the results and the children can write them down. The results can be shown as a bar chart.

Pushing and pulling as hard as we can involves arms, legs and body, so total weight can aid the strength of muscles. When the charts are completed, discuss with the children whether they think there is any relationship between the best pushers and pullers and their height and weight.

Copymasters

Use copymaster 58 (Pushing and pulling) to record what the children had to do in a given activity, by drawing a tick in the appropriate box. The space at the bottom is used to record the child's name and the strength of his or her push and pull.

Purpose

To show that pushes and pulls can make things start moving and speed up.

Materials needed

Socks, plimsolls, large box, broom handles or wooden rounders posts, skateboards, roller boots, bicycle, scooter, pull-along toys, large sit-upon toys, large water trough, toy boats.

Activity 1

Using a PE lesson, ask the children what it feels like when we push or pull bare feet along the floor.

Beware of splinters and ask the children to push feet gently.

Next ask the children to put on their socks and repeat the action. Ask them which was the easiest to do. Last of all ask the children to put on plimsolls, training or outdoor shoes and to decide whether these make pushing and pulling easier.

Activity 2

The children can try to push or pull a variety of objects across the floor. Make sure that some objects are flat bottomed and some others have wheels. The children can sort the objects into easy movers and difficult movers and you can discuss with them if there are any similarities between the two groups and within the two groups.

Activity 3

Take a large box and get one child to sit inside and two other children to push or pull it across the floor. When they have tried to do this, use the wooden posts or broom handles and place them under the box. Does the box move more easily now?

Activity 4

Get the children to bring into school some of the toys mentioned under 'Materials needed' above. They can decide what is needed to start moving e.g. toy cars, skateboards, roller boots, bicycle, scooter, the pull-along toys and the clockwork toys that need to be pulled backwards in order to engage the mechanism that makes them move forwards. Some of the large sit-upon toys will also be useful for this exercise.

On a smooth horizontal surface the children can try pushing each object gently to see how far it goes and how fast it moves. They can then push them harder and finally, as hard as possible, to see if they move farther and faster.

Use the sit-upon toddler toys and see what action is needed to start them moving. Once the toy has started moving does it need pushing as hard or as often?

Activity 5

Take the children to the playground of the local park. Try pushing the roundabout gently and ask the children if it moves fast or slowly. Try pushing it as hard as you can and observe whether it moves faster. Does it need an extra hard push to get it going? The children can see whether they need to keep pushing the roundabout in order to maintain the speed and what happens when they stop pushing.

Activity 6

Now try the swings. Pull the swing back a little way and let go. Encourage the children to notice the distance and height of the swing and also the speed.

See what happens when you pull the swing back further. Does it swing faster or higher? Finally try giving the hardest push possible. If a visit to the park is not possible or there are no swings, you can set up a pendulum using string and Plasticine® hanging from the top of an open doorway.

Activity 7

Take a variety of objects, some heavy such as a large block of wood or a large thick book and some light things such as an inflated balloon, a paper bag, a ping-pong ball or a marble. Mark out a large rectangle on a smooth, flat surface and place the objects at one end.

The children can then see how many gentle pushes are needed to move the object the full length of the rectangle. They can then repeat this and see how many hard pushes were needed to take the object the same distance.

Activity 8

Extra pushes can make an object speed up. The children can try pushing a toy boat across the surface of the water in the water trough. At first it will travel quickly but then it will slow down. Another push will make it speed up again and so on.

Copymasters

Use copymaster 59 (How things move when pushed) to show how strength of push affects speed of movement, whether the objects continue moving after they have been pushed or whether they stop moving as soon as they are not being pushed. The children put a tick in the appropriate column and there is also a space to record the distance travelled after one push.

The sheet can also be used to test the effectiveness of one push along a flat surface, an uphill slope and a downhill slope. The slope used can be shown by colouring in the appropriate box.

 Area of study 3 | **SWERVING AND STOPPING** | C60

Purpose

To show that pushes and pulls can cause things to swerve or stop.

Materials needed

Hose pipe, squeezy bottle, toy car, marbles, ping-pong ball, Smartie tube, toy boat, hairdryer, ink, drinking straws, skateboard, handkerchief, string, weight, Plasticine®, a selection of materials to build barriers, e.g. matchboxes, stones, house bricks, Lego® or Duplo® bricks, books.

Activity 1

Talk about pushes and pulls which affect us. In the PE lesson children can walk around the hall and they can try pushing and pulling their friends to try and make them change direction.

Activity 2

Look at which can push and pull: body power, moving air and moving water.

Take the children outside and set up a series of simple tests. Use a hose pipe or more simply a squeezy bottle filled with water. Choose several different objects, such as a toy car, a marble, an empty Smartie tube, a full Smartie tube, a ping-pong ball, a skateboard. Working in twos or in small groups, one child is to pull or push the object in one direction while the other aims the jet of water at it from another direction to try to make it swerve or stop.

Moving air can also be used to cause the object to swerve or stop. The same tests can be repeated but this time a hairdryer can be used or, if it is a very windy day, the wind itself may be strong enough to cause a swerve or stop.

Activity 3

The effect of the wind on the course of a toy sailing boat can be seen quite effectively using a large tank of water, a toy boat and a hairdryer.

One child pushes the boat forwards and the jet of air can be aimed at the boat from different directions to see what happens. (The same sort of effect can be seen when playing blow football or by using the technique of blowing a blob of ink or paint with a drinking straw to make a design.)

Remember the dangers of using electrical appliances near water. Hairdryers should always be used by an adult.

Activity 4

Paper darts can be made to swerve or change direction by using a hairdryer aimed across the flight path. Balloons and ping-pong balls can also be used if they are rolled across the floor.

Activity 5

The effect of pulling can be observed by making a toy parachute. Throw a reasonably heavy object up into the air (e.g. a key) and let the children watch how it falls. Then make a parachute by tying a string to each of the four corners of a piece of light cloth and then tying these strings to the key. Then throw the key up into the air again and let the children observe how the key falls this time.

The parachute pulls against the air and slows down the descent. In the calm of the classroom, the key should fall vertically, but go outside on a windy day and repeat the flight to see if the cross winds make any difference to the descent.

Activity 6

Flying a kite on a windy day can also demonstrate how the pushes and pulls of the wind make the kite swerve and stop.

Activity 7

An anchor can be used to make a toy car slow down and stop. Set up a ramp and roll a toy car from the top. See how fast it goes and how far it travels.

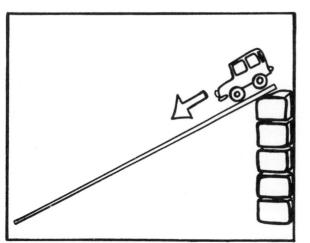

Now attach a parachute to the back of the car and let the car roll down the slope again. Hold the end of the parachute as you let the car go so that it opens. Ask the children whether the car travels as far or as fast.

Activity 8

Another way to make an anchor is to attach the car to a piece of Plasticine® with string. The car will continue to travel forward as long as there is enough play in the string. As soon as the string is fully extended the weight of the Plasticine® will pull the car to a standstill. The children may need to experiment to find the optimum amount of Plasticine® to use.

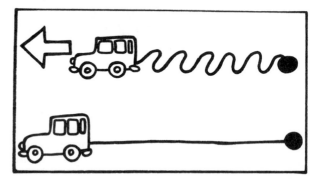

Activity 9

An object will stop if it meets a barrier that is stronger than itself or the energy it has to move itself forwards.

Using different materials the children can set up barriers to test which is the most effective at stopping a given object. The children can try different strength pushes to see if the harder they push the easier it is to break the barrier or not.

Copymasters

Use copymaster 60 (Trying to make objects swerve) to test the effect of wind and water power on the movement of the objects listed. Children can tick the appropriate column and colour the hose pipe or the hairdryer depending on what they used to try and effect a swerve.

Attainment target 11: Electricity and magnetism

Pupils should develop their knowledge and understanding of electric and electromagnetic effects in simple circuits, electric devices and domestic appliances.

Level 2	**Statements of attainment**

Pupils should:

- know that magnets attract certain materials but not others and can repel each other.
- understand the danger associated with the use of electricity, and know appropriate safety measures.

Area of study 1

MAGNETS ATTRACT

C61

Purpose
To show that magnets attract certain materials but not others.

Materials needed
An assortment of magnets of different sizes and shapes, paper, pens, scissors, glue, card, cardboard boxes, an assortment of metal objects (spoons, pins, tin plates, screws, pens, tins, badges, toys, springs, foil, wire, piping); examples of animal, vegetable and mineral material (e.g. fur, fabrics, wood, plants, glass, rocks and ores, and man-made materials such as plastics); water and a large container.

Be careful to exclude metal and other objects that are rusty, sharp or poisonous.

Activity 1: Investigate the power of a magnet
Let the children explore all the materials you have collected and see whether the magnets will attract any of them. Try things belonging to the children, such as belt buckles, pencil cases, combs, bags, clothes. You may feel you can loan some precious metal such as a ring or a chain for brief investigation. You will quickly make two sets: things which are attracted to magnets and things which are not. The children may notice that all of the things attracted to a magnet are metal, but that not all metals are attracted to a magnet. (In order to be attracted metal objects must have some iron content.)

Activity 2
Display new vocabulary as it comes up in conversation, such as metal, magnet, iron, steel, aluminium, brass, bronze, lead, copper, gold, silver, tin, platinum, attract, repel, poles, compass, north, south, force.

black activity paper

red paper

white paper 'force field'

force repel
attract tin south
pole iron north
metal steel

Activity 3: Make a fishing game
This will show that some metals are attracted to magnets.

paper clip

Fishing game

cane

card

card circle approx. 30 cm diameter

wool or light string

magnet

Decorate with felt pens.

Give each fish a number under 10 and let the children total their own 'catch' to find the winner of the game.

67

Activity 4: Build with magnets

Magnetise metal bolts, screws, bits of wire, strips of metal and so on by stroking them gently in one direction with a strong magnet. You can then stick these magnetised bits to each other to make magnetic sculptures.

Build with magnets

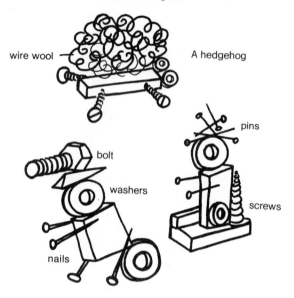

Activity 5: Can magnets work through things?

Test the power of magnets to attract through other materials. Try materials such as plastics, glass, wood, card and items which can be rigid.

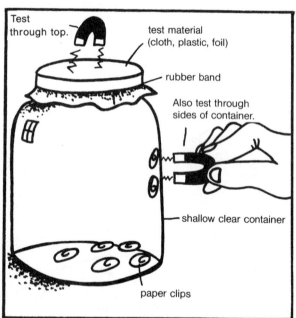

Try the power of a magnet through water, either by immersing both the magnet and the metal things in a large bowl or by keeping the magnet outside to see if it will attract through the side of the bowl and through the water.

Activity 6: Make a race track

Use a large flat cardboard box with two sides cut out. Make 'power' sticks as shown, and using toy cars have a race round the track.

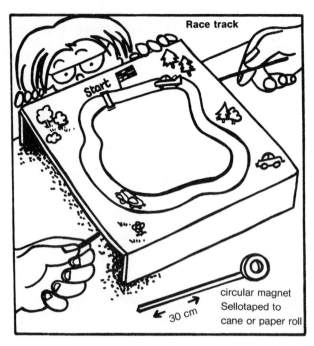

Race track

circular magnet
Sellotaped to
cane or paper roll

30 cm

Activity 7: Make magnetic football

Make 'power' sticks as for the race game, using quite powerful magnets. Make three to four players for each team, using card stuck to flat round corks. Put three drawing pins in the base of each. The football field can be made from a large flat cardboard box, decorated appropriately.

Activity 8: Magnet energy can lift

How strong is your magnet? Make a paper clip chain. Small items such as paper clips are easily magnetised. See how many you can make into a chain. Have a competition to find the longest chain.

Activity 9: A hanging chain

Use a box as a base and rest a bar magnet on the edge, weighting it down with a book or some other non-metal object. See how many paper clips you can hang from it.

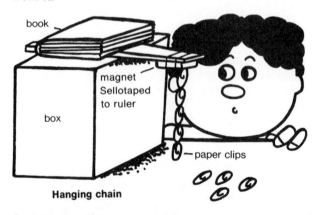

book

magnet
Sellotaped
to ruler

box

paper clips

Hanging chain

Activity 10: Flying paper clips

Set up the test as shown on page 69 and see how far from the edge of your magnet its force extends. Pull the paper clip to its fullest extent and note when the attraction is broken. Lay the clip on the table and pull it around without the magnet touching the clip.

Magnetic energy is used in real life in many ways. In scrapyards giant magnets lifted by cranes move old

magnet
paper clip
cotton
Sellotape

cars and scrap as easily as the children's magnets lift paper clips.

Copymasters

Use copymaster 61 (Guess what) to record a simple sorting activity, using magnetism. Give small groups of children five small items or pieces of materials and ask them to test each one to see if it is attracted by magnetism. Ask the children first to make a guess and then to test their idea and record it appropriately. Use bits of thin card, wood, wool, fabric, plastic, rubber, pins, paper clips, foil, wire and so on, which can be stuck to the test sheet with a quick drying glue such as Copydex®.

 Area of study 2

MAGNETS REPEL

 C62

Purpose

To show that magnets have opposite and like poles and that like poles repel each other, whilst unlike poles attract each other.

Materials needed

White art paper or card, greetings card boxes, powder paint, iron filings, a selection of magnets (horse shoe, bar, circular), pastel fixative, a piece of glass about 30 cm square with the edges smoothed, nylon thread, a selection of compasses.

Activity 1

Show that magnets have a force field around them and that this magnetic field varies according to the shape of the magnet.

Place a bar magnet on a table and put a small piece of card on top of it. Scatter iron filings on top of the card and tap it lightly with the forefinger. Watch them form into the shape of the magnetic field. Remove the magnet from underneath and watch the field disintegrate. Iron filings are notoriously energetic so it is a good idea to use a greetings card box for this experiment.

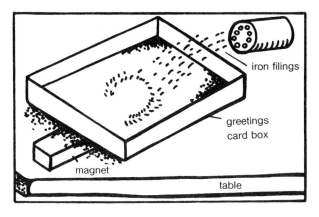

iron filings

greetings card box

magnet

table

See what different shapes of magnetic field form around the different shaped magnets. The children can try to draw these from direct observation.

Activity 2

If you are careful it is possible to fix the pattern of iron filings. Mix some filings with dry powder paint to give an extra colour dimension and make the magnetic field as above. Use a pastel fixative sprayed lightly from at least 30 cm above to fix the filings and paint whilst not disturbing the field. This method at least fixes the filings so that the magnet can be removed from underneath and the pattern observed for a short while.

Activity 3

Magnets have two poles. Let the children experiment on the table top using pairs of magnets. They should notice that certain ends of the magnets will be attracted to each other whilst others actively repel each other. Try pushing one magnet with another using this power of repulsion. Children with the toy railway made by Brio will know about this power, if not the cause of it, as the trucks on the train each have a magnet inside and are coupled by the magnets' force or repulsed as the case may be.

Activity 4

Tell the children that the two poles are called north and south. In actual fact the north pole is a 'north seeking pole'. The poles are usually marked on a magnet. If a bar magnet is suspended freely, it will point to the Earth's magnetic north.

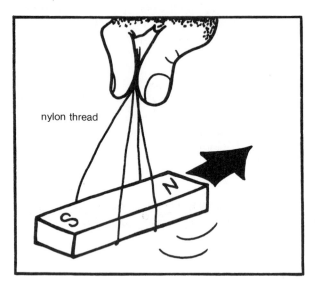

The north gives a starting position from which directions can be given. This magnetic north is about 8° west of the actual geographic north pole.

Activity 5

Mark where north is from your classroom and make a simple compass, by finding north with a suspended magnet and marking the point on a sheet of paper on the floor. Then mark out the other three points and fix to the floor using a sheet of sticky-backed plastic. Mark these directions on the wall and make up games involving changing direction using the points of the compass.

Activity 6

Use the piece of glass to show the magnetic field with iron filings using one bar magnet. Put another bar magnet in the position shown and watch the filings

move along the lines of force. Move the magnets with like poles facing and note the pattern of repulsion shown by the magnetic field. The unlike poles will be attracted, but the weight of the glass will prevent them from turning.

Activity 7

Hang two bar magnets side by side with the like poles together and then the unlike poles together. What do you notice?

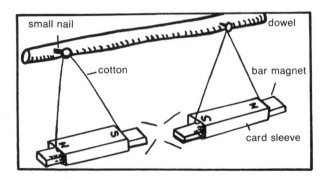

Copymasters

Use copymaster 62 (Magnetic poles) to record this area of study. There are three combinations of pairs of magnets with the poles in different combinations and the children are asked to guess what will happen and test what happened in each case. The children can write short sentences to record.

DANGER AND SAFETY

Purpose

To show that electricity can be dangerous and to make children aware of safety measures.

Materials needed

CEGB video 'Play safe', pictures and photographs of different electrical equipment used at home and in school (office, classroom, kitchen and caretaker's equipment).

Activity 1

Watch the video 'Play safe' as recommended in Level 1 AT11 (see page 22). It is particularly suitable for older children who become more adventurous as they explore their neighbourhood.

Activity 2

Talk about the dangers associated with misuse of electricity. Make a list of dangers, e.g. faulty flex, sockets near water supply, poking things into sockets, wet hands near electrical equipment, flex trailing across floor, overloading sockets with adaptors and so on.

Activity 3

Paint posters warning of these and other dangers you and the children think of. Put them up around school.

Activity 4

Devise a safety scale for your school with all the dangers you can think of listed. Give points for each according to the degree of danger, e.g. faulty flex could score two, wet hands on equipment could score five, equipment standing in water scores 10 and so on. If you have a pylon or sub-station in or near the school grounds, make playing near these worth 20!

Send teams of children round the school to conduct the safety survey, looking in all areas, including the staff room, head's office, caretaker's room and so on. Obviously the children may need to be accompanied by an adult in places such as the boiler house or the caretaker's room where dangerous things are stored.

At the end of the survey collate the results on to a master chart and award a poster for the safest room in school. Put danger warnings near hazards.

Activity 6

Give simple first aid training on what to do for electric shock. Stress the importance of not touching the victim if there is any sort of explosion and an adult is not around. Children must not touch equipment in this case, although an adult should disconnect the supply. Once this is done the victim should be reassured if conscious and kept warm, and an ambulance should be sent for. If unconscious, resuscitation may be needed if there is no pulse. Check first aid training for all adults in school on a regular basis. The ambulance service will come into school and train staff in resuscitation techniques and will often be willing to train young children also.

The most important thing for the children to know in the case of possible electrocution is not to touch and to get adult help. You may want to teach the children how to make a 999 call.

Activity 7

Look into other safety procedures in school. Ask the fire service to come in to do a check on fire hazards specially for your class or ask to accompany them on a routine check. Find out about the school's fire drill and organise one if you do not have them on a regular basis. Discuss the procedure with the children afterwards and see if they can identify any improvements which are needed.

Copymasters

Use copymaster 63 (Danger) to consolidate the learning in this Area of Study. The children have to match the picture of the hazard with the sentence describing it.

Attainment target 12: The scientific aspects of information technology including microelectronics

Pupils should develop their knowledge and understanding of information transfer and microelectronics.

Level 2	**Statements of attainment**

Pupils should:

- know that there is a variety of means for communicating information over long distances.
- know that information can be stored using a range of everyday devices, including the computer.

Area of study 1	**VISUAL COMMUNICATION**	C64

Purpose
To identify visually the variety of means of communicating information over long distances.

Materials needed
Photographs of the following (or the actual items): television (with Teletext), word processor, video recorder, video camera, computer, fax machine, camera, calculator; pictures of information boards such as at airports and railway stations.

Activity 1
Try to bring in as many of the machines as possible or at least photographs of them and talk about the kind of information they communicate.

Mention the fact that all these machines use electricity to either pick up or transmit a signal which contains information and most of them need an aerial or cable to do this.

The children will have seen satellite dishes on buildings and some may even have one on their home. It is not necessary to explain how one of these machines works at this stage, but merely to show what happens, for example, when a programme is transmitted. This can be done by means of a simple illustration (see below).

Satellites high above the earth are used to help signals to travel longer distances between countries and continents.

Activity 2
Set up an electrical store in the role-play corner and make some models of the different appliances or collect old unusable ones for the children to sell. They will soon become familiar with the names of the different machines. Try to obtain some of the brochures from stores and shops. This will also help recognition.

Activity 3
Use some of the machines in the classroom so that the children can actually see how they work. They probably watch the schools' programmes on ITV and BBC so there is a prime example of information being communicated over long distances. Even though sound is part of the broadcast, in this case the image is the prime means of communicating information.

Look at the Teletext pages of Ceefax and Oracle and using the index page give the children hands on experience of how to call up the various information pages by pressing the buttons on the remote control.

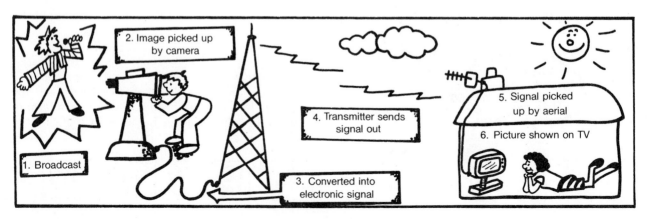

1. Broadcast
2. Image picked up by camera
3. Converted into electronic signal
4. Transmitter sends signal out
5. Signal picked up by aerial
6. Picture shown on TV

The jokes pages will be popular. Some programmes have subtitles for the hard of hearing and the Ceefax and Oracle pages can be used to superimpose the subtitles at the bottom of the television screen. The children will enjoy calling up these pages using the remote control.

Activity 4
It may be that some of the parents have or have access to a fax machine and they may be able to come in and talk about how it works. Try to obtain some of the printouts so that the children can see what the transmitted information looks like.

Activity 5
Use the video camera to record a piece of information. The children might pretend to be reporters sending the latest news from somewhere in the world. This will give them an insight into how the news from all over the globe is collected, edited and compiled as their regular evening news spot on television. This can be compared to the old reel film which needed to be processed and then shown using a projector.

Activity 6
Give the children access to a computer and let them look at the information which can be stored on it. Show them that the software is important but that much information can be stored in the conventional way, in the memory.

Look at word processors as well and show the children how the text can be shifted or rearranged if necessary. The software is a convenient size for posting to anywhere in the world and information can be easily retrieved on another computer.

Activity 7
The hazard warning lights on the motorways are controlled from area control boxes and information and warnings can be passed down the motorway to warn motorists of potential hazards such as fog or lane closure. Many of the children may have seen these lights and wondered how they work. They may try to devise their own system of lights or signals to pass on information over a given distance. The simplest of these are coloured lights, e.g. if the light is green, go ahead; if it is red, stop; if it is yellow, slow down now and so on. You could use torches with coloured Cellophane over the end to illustrate this.

Copymasters
Use copymaster 64 (Passing on visual information) to record the time and place they saw the machine illustrated, by writing in the spaces next to each picture.

AUDIO COMMUNICATION

C65

Purpose
To identify the variety of ways audio information is passed over long distances.

Materials needed
Photographs (and/or the actual machines) of: tape recorder, telephone, record player, CD player, satellite dish.

Activity 1
Use the photographs in the same way as for Area of Study 1 but this time focus on the spoken word or the sounds that are transmitted.

Of these machines, the radio is probably the most familiar to the children and once again, a simple illustration to show how the information is transmitted and picked up will help them (see below).

Let the children handle the radio so that they can see how it works. Look for the on/off switch and the programme selector and tuner. They will have fun tuning into foreign stations which will again show how far some of the radio signals have travelled. Some radios show quite well how direction is important when picking up a signal, e.g. the signal will be a lot stronger when the radio is facing in one direction rather than in another. The importance of the aerial can be shown by extending it to receive the best signal and by seeing what happens when the aerial is pushed down.

Activity 2
Most of the children will have a telephone or will at least have seen one. Explain how the telephone is used and possibly give them practice on an old model in the

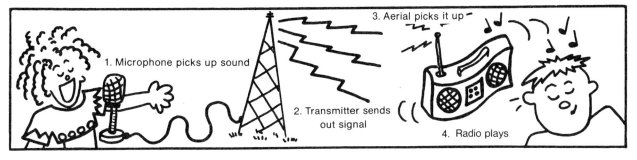

1. Microphone picks up sound
2. Transmitter sends out signal
3. Aerial picks it up
4. Radio plays

role-play corner, or even actually let them use one in the school office. You could arrange to phone a class in another school or even one of the parents. Talk about each telephone having its own number so that if the number is dialled correctly we should be able to pass on and receive information whenever we want to.

Talk about some of the information services offered by Telecom, such as the weather, travel news, cricket scores, gardening tips and jokes. Look in the directory for the numbers and let the children try dialling them. Do warn against misuse of the 999 system.

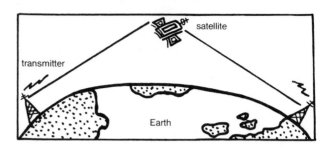

Activity 3

Use the school tape recorder to record the children reading one of their stories or reciting a poem. Show them how it works and let the whole class have a turn at saying something into the tape recorder. Link this to the study of the record player and show them how information/entertainment is passed on using tape and record. These machines come in portable sizes and all that is needed to gain access to the information stored is another machine of the same kind.

Activity 4

Satellites are also used for transmitting signals from one country to another and different satellites are used for radio, telephone and fax machines. The satellites are used to overcome the problem of the curvature of the earth. Make a simple model using a large ball.

Look at radio phones and car phones and the radios used by the emergency services. Try and arrange a visit to the local police station and see how they communicate with traffic cars and policemen and policewomen out on the beat. Alternatively, try to arrange for one of the emergency services to visit school, bringing their radios with them. They may be able to arrange for the children to listen to them communicating with their control section.

Activity 5

Look at the telegraph system and Morse code. The children can devise their own system of sounds to mean different things, the simplest being one knock for 'yes' and two knocks for 'no'.

Copymasters

Use copymaster 65 (Passing on audio information) to record the time and place the machines illustrated were seen, by writing in the spaces next to each picture.

 STORING INFORMATION

Purpose
To identify how information is stored.

Materials needed
All the pictures and machines from the first two Areas of Study, a selection of audio cassette tapes, audio and visual floppy discs for computer, computer games, compact disc records and vinyl records (45s and LPs), a selection of food containers showing the bar code, magnet.

Activity 1
Look at all the machines from Areas of Study 1 and 2 and let the children sort them into groups of those which receive information and transmit it, those which merely play stored information and those which can be fed information from whatever source, store it and then retrieve it at a later date. The sorting will involve much discussion and your help is essential.

Activity 2
Set up a display of the three main groups and then look at the way the information is stored. Look at the video recorder and the audio cassette tape it needs to store

the information. If possible use a video camera to store some action in the classroom, so that the children can watch the action happen, observe someone recording it with the camera and then watch the replay through the video recorder and the TV.

Activity 3
Repeat Activity 2 using a tape recorder so that the children can see what is needed to record the voice. To show that the information is stored on a tape in both cases, try to record something without using a cassette.

Use the school record player and listen to and look at the records played on it. Look at the surface of the record through a magnifying glass so that the children will see the ridges and grooves. Compare these with the surface of a compact disc or a floppy disc. Look into the differences between a CD player and a record player.

Activity 4
Set up the school computer and show the children how they can type information onto the screen and store it on the floppy disc. Again, test this by trying to store information without a disc.

Activity 5

With all these machines a disc or tape is needed and many of these tapes are magnetic tapes.

A simple experiment can show this. Take a video or audio tape and record something on it and play it back so that the children can see or hear it. Eject the tape and run a magnet along the exposed tape at the top. Now try to play it back and see what happens. The magnet will have mixed up the recorded signal on the tape and the recording will be spoiled. Remember to keep the magnet away from any tapes you wish to keep intact.

Activity 6

Use the collection of food boxes and containers and look for the bar codes to be found on all of them. Many of the children will have seen how the person at the supermarket checkout uses these with the till. No buttons are needed to put in information about the product; it is passed on visually. The product name and price comes up on the till's screen. The children could collect different examples of receipts from computerised tills to show how computers are everywhere in our lives.

Activity 7

Computers store a variety of information such as names and addresses, TV and radio times, doctors's records, bank statements, bills and invoices. The whole world of entertainment has changed with records, video films, and stories on cassette. The use of the instant replay facility can show again and again a piece of sporting or historic action.

The children might like to make or plan a time capsule of the 1990s containing things which show how we live today. They would need to think how to store the information and whether to put in one of the machines needed to play the recordings.

Copymasters

Use copymaster 66 (Storing information). This is a simple matching exercise, to match machine to storage method.

Attainment target 13: Energy

Pupils should develop their knowledge and understanding of the nature of energy, its transfer and control.

They should develop their knowledge and understanding of the range of energy sources and the issues involved in their exploitation.

Level 2

Statements of attainment

Pupils should:

- understand the meaning of 'hot' and 'cold' relative to the temperature of their own bodies.
- be able to describe how a toy with a simple mechanism which moves and stores energy works.

Area of study 1

HOT AND COLD

 C67

Purpose

To help children to understand the meaning of 'hot' and 'cold'.

Materials needed

A selection of children's clothes for all seasons, pictures of different types of weather, pictures of different heating and cooling equipment, such as fans, fires, radiators, paper, pens, scissors, glue, ice, thermometers, concentrated fruit flavours for ice lollies.

Activity 1

Discuss what things make the children feel hot or cold and make two lists. You can use copymaster 67 enlarged to A3 size for this initial discussion. You may get answers such as 'my jumper, my duvet, the Sun, the fire make me hot', or 'ice lollies, cold water, the wind make me cold'. Try to organise the items into sets with the children. You may find them under the headings of the following activities, but if not you can introduce them.

Activity 2: Clothes

Talk about what the weather feels like at different times of the year and the need for clothes which keep our bodies feeling neither too hot nor too cold. Make a collection of clothes that make us warmer and clothes that make us cooler. Cut out appropriate clothes from magazines and display them in sets.

Investigate colour and temperature. Do dark colours make us feel warmer and do light colours make us feel cooler? Try this out in the summer. Light colours reflect the Sun's rays to a certain extent.

Investigate the insulation properties of clothes. Try a simple experiment to see what materials are most efficient at keeping in the heat. Make cloaks of different materials for children to wear on a cold day. Let everyone have a go in the different types and get a consensus of opinion on the warmest through to the least warm. Use materials such as newspaper, cardboard, wool, cotton, nylon, fur, plastic, a duvet, a blanket and if you can obtain one, a silver survival blanket of the kind used in rescue.

Activity 3: Movement
During a PE lesson, possibly outside, get the children to work so hard that they feel hot. Talk about how the movement energy they expended produced heat in their bodies. They will already know that if they are cold, fast movement warms them. Shivering is the body's way of moving the muscles if they are too cold. Show them how to cool down by walking round. Ask such questions as: What do you feel like doing now? What will make you feel cool? Would you like to sit near the fire?

Activity 4: Weather
Talk about the weather today and how the children feel. Ask such questions as: Will you need your coats at playtime? What does the sun feel like in winter/summer? What does the wind make you feel? Does rain make you feel warm? Does snow make you feel warm? Have you ever had sunburn?

This should promote a lot of discussion as younger children sometimes confuse warmth caused by their body's movement with the temperature of the weather, for example, 'Snow makes me warm'. Go outside and experiment with the temperature of the day.

Identify the sources of different temperatures in the weather, i.e. the Sun as the major source of heat, the cooling effect of the wind. Discuss temperatures at night-time when the Sun has gone down.

Activity 5: Artificial heat sources
Talk about the methods used to heat the children's homes. Look round school to see how many different heating and cooling methods are used, from boiler to open windows.

Activity 6: The body
All the above systems have an effect on our body. The skin is the body's heating and cooling system. Talk about sweating and shivering as normal processes to keep body temperature even. Sometimes when we are ill this gets disturbed and we feel cold when we are in a warm room and a warm bed, or we get over hot in cool conditions. Are all skins the same? Do children with black skins get sunburnt like white skinned children?

Make a fan. Try out several shapes of hand fan to see which is the most effective in cooling. Use different types of paper and card and make them in different sizes. You may need to heat up some children (by sending them to run round the playground until they are hot!) in order to conduct the experiment.

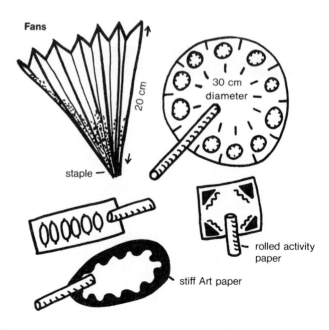

Fans

76

Activity 7

Food fuels the body and certain foods, such as carbohydrates and fats, help to keep us warm in winter. Talk about favourite foods in different seasons. Try out some recipes. You could simply try drinking hot drinks on a hot day and cold drinks on a cold day and discuss with the children what these drinks make them feel like. Then try the usual drink for the weather.

Make ice lollies whatever the season and use different flavours of fruit concentrate. Have a survey to see which flavour is the most thirst quenching. Is thirst connected to being hot?

Copymasters

Use copymaster 67 (Hot and cold) to record this Area of Study. Children can make personal lists of the things which make them hot or cold or they can draw pictures of these things or stick on pictures cut from magazines.

MECHANICAL TOYS THAT WORK

Purpose

To show the children how simple mechanisms that move and store energy work.

Materials needed

Card tubes, flat card, paper, glues, scissors, pens, string or wool, cotton reels, matchboxes, rubber bands, a collection of small mechanical toys.

Activity 1: A spinner

Prepare the spinner as shown in AT15 Level 1. To work the toy, throw the card over and over until the wool is tightly twisted and then pull each end simultaneously and gently to make the circle spin and hum.

In this case movement energy in the form of a spring made of wool is stored until the two ends are pulled. It is possible to keep this spinner moving for quite a while by gently releasing and winding the wool by the action.

Activity 2: A roundabout

Construct as shown below but be sure to use a fairly heavy wood base or weigh down a lighter one. The lolly sticks are used to turn the tube on the roundabout which winds up in the string. The tube on the block is fixed in position and acts as a slip for the weighted string. Experiment to find a good weight of Plasticine®, depending on how fast you want the roundabout to go.

Activity 3: Cotton reel tank

Build this as shown overleaf. You will need a smooth, flat surface on which to run this toy. The hall floor may be most suitable as it can go considerable distances. Make several and have distance trials, introducing variables such as a standard number of turns, a rough road (the outside path), different sized reels.

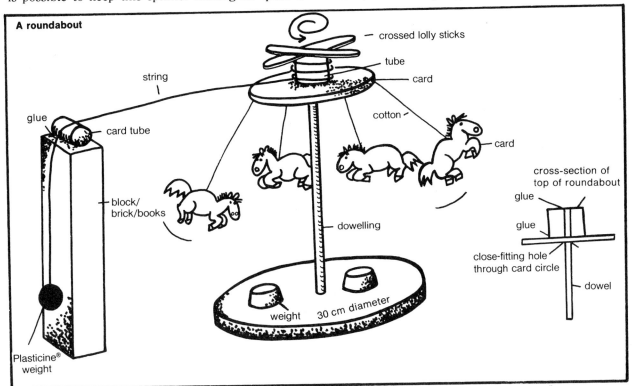

A roundabout

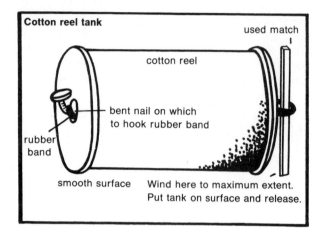

Cotton reel tank

used match

cotton reel

bent nail on which to hook rubber band

rubber band

smooth surface

Wind here to maximum extent. Put tank on surface and release.

Activity 4: A matchbox boat

Construct as shown, but use as long a container as possible for the water trials as sometimes boats can go quite far.

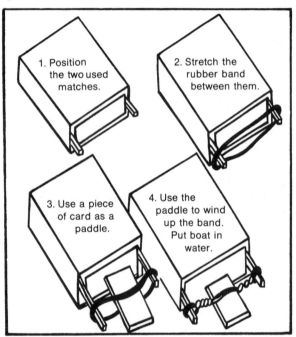

1. Position the two used matches.

2. Stretch the rubber band between them.

3. Use a piece of card as a paddle.

4. Use the paddle to wind up the band. Put boat in water.

Activity 5: Ready-made toys

Make a collection of simple moving toys such as a yo-yo, clockwork bath frogs, boats and divers and spring powered pets. Play with them extensively and even dismantle a few in order to find out how they work. Discuss the concept of energy stored in devices such as springs, rubber bands, etc. Try replacing the yo-yo's twisted string with untwisted wool or nylon thread. What happens? Will the yo-yo still work?

Spring-powered pets

rubber sucker

head pressed down, spring temporarily coiled tight to be released when suction gives out

Copymasters

Use copymaster 68 (The amazing...) to record the making of one of these toys or any other you have made. The children can fill in the end of the title themselves. They can draw the toy and then draw each stage in its construction in the correct sequence. Children can write comments in any empty boxes. If there are not enough boxes use another sheet, cutting off the top section.

 Area of study 3

OTHER TOYS THAT WORK

 C69

Purpose

To show children how simple mechanisms that move and store energy work.

Materials needed

Margarine tubs, balloons, polystyrene food trays, metal cigar tube, firm wire, night-light, washing-up liquid bottle, cork, plastic straw, Plasticine®, vinegar, baking soda, water, tissue paper, glue, scissors.

Activity 1: A hovercraft

Cut a small hole in the base of a margarine tub and push through the end of a balloon. To power the hovercraft, blow up the balloon as it is, in position. Then release it on a smooth surface and watch it skim around. The air stored in the balloon is the power source.

Blow.

Activity 2: A gas-powered boat

Prepare the boat and its fuel as shown. Cork the end of the bottle and give it a shake to mix the baking soda and the vinegar and quickly place it on the water. You will need a long water tray or a baby bath. A gas is produced when the vinegar and baking soda combine and as this escapes through the small hole of the straw it pushes the boat along.

Activity 3: A steam-powered boat

Make the boat as shown and position it on the water before lighting the night-light. As the water in the tube boils it will turn into steam and as this escapes from the straw, the boat is pushed along.

Copymasters

Use copymaster 69 (I made a . . .) to record how the children made one of these toys or any other you think of. The children can draw the toy and then explain in words what materials they used, how they made it and what happened when they used it.

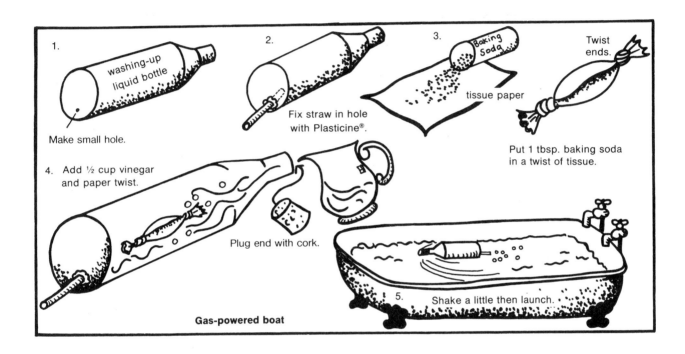

1. washing-up liquid bottle
Make small hole.

2. Fix straw in hole with Plasticine®.

3. Baking Soda
tissue paper
Twist ends.
Put 1 tbsp. baking soda in a twist of tissue.

4. Add ½ cup vinegar and paper twist.
Plug end with cork.

5. Shake a little then launch.

Gas-powered boat

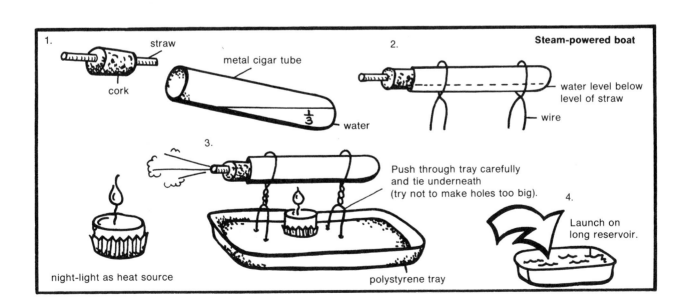

1. straw
cork

metal cigar tube
$\frac{1}{3}$
water

Steam-powered boat

2. water level below level of straw
wire

3. Push through tray carefully and tie underneath (try not to make holes too big).

night-light as heat source

polystyrene tray

4. Launch on long reservoir.

Attainment target 14: Sound and music

Pupils should develop their knowledge and understanding of the properties, transmission and absorption of sound.

Level 2

Statements of attainment

Pupils should:

- know that sounds are heard when the sound reaches the ear.
- be able to explain how musical sounds are produced in simple musical instruments.

Area of study 1

HEARING SOUNDS

C70

Purpose
To show that sound is heard when it reaches the ear.

Materials needed
Tape recorder, glass, pencil, paper bag, bottle of water, sheets of sandpaper, drawing pins, tin lid, cotton wool, ear defenders, personal cassette with headphones, drum, paper and pencils.

Activity 1
Sit still and listen to the sounds all around. After two minutes ask the children to name all the sounds they heard. Try to sort them into sets of high and low sounds or loud and quiet noises.

Try this in a variety of locations, for example, classroom, playground, the side of a busy road, a garden or any other place which might be suitable.

Activity 2
Make a recording of four or five different sounds all being made at the same time and ask the children to try and identify the things which were making the noises, for example, banging a glass with a pencil, rustling paper, rubbing sandpaper sheets together, bursting a paper bag, pouring liquid from a bottle. This should prove that it is easier to identify separate sounds.

Activity 3
Test to see how far away you can hear things. Working in pairs, test how well the sound of a pin being dropped can be heard. Decide what height the pin will be dropped from and what surface it will be dropped on to. One child stands behind the other but quite a distance away. Drop the pin from a height of 1 cm on to a tin lid. The child holding the lid is to move forward one pace at a time, dropping the pin as before at each stop. As soon as the partner can hear the pin drop, he/she should raise his/her hand. The distance is then measured.

The experiment can then be repeated, this time dropping the pin from a height of 5 cm, then 10 cm. Try this with several children: the one who hears the pin drop at the greatest distance has the most acute hearing.

Activity 4
Try listening to someone speaking quietly when you are close to them. Move away until you cannot hear them at all. Measure the distance, then test several children.

Activity 5
Test what happens when you try to stop sound reaching your ears. Which of these methods is most successful: a) hands over ears, b) cotton wool in the ears, c) wearing ear defenders, d) wearing a personal stereo headphone set, with music?

Ask one of the children to beat a drum and see which method is most effective at blocking the noise. (The music is most effective because it fills the ear with a louder noise.) Explain that it is dangerous to wear Walkman® headphones in the street because it is difficult to hear traffic. Talk about excessive noise as a danger to health, e.g. in factories where huge noise makes it difficult to hear speech. Also mention noise pollution from motorways and airports.

Activity 6
Can sound go round corners and through walls? Send small groups of children into the corridor, behind a wall, outside the window, behind a door, behind a curtain, and ask them to make some loud noise (by arrangement with neighbouring classes!). See how well it can be heard. Make up a simple scale of noise level: hear well, quite well, not very well, not at all.

Copymasters
Use copymaster 70 (Hearing sounds) to test how well children can hear the various sounds at close range, from a distance, in another room, and when there is other noise. Write the appropriate response in each box.

CATCHING SOUNDS

Area of study 2 — C71

Purpose
To show that certain objects can help the ear to pick up sounds.

Materials needed
Bell, ear defenders, card, plastic tube and two funnels, watch and a length of wood, two cans or yoghurt cartons and a length of string or wire, whistle, triangle, cymbals, trundle wheel.

Activity 1: Which direction is the sound coming from?
Test how well children can identify the direction of a sound. Children sit blindfolded in a chair, one at a time, with the head pointing forwards. Ring a bell in front of the child at chest height. See if the child can point to the bell. Now try ringing the bell in other positions, left, right, behind, above, The children can record the number of correct guesses and the direction on a chart like this:

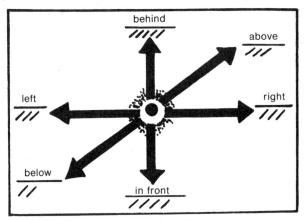

Try the same experiment but this time cover up one ear at a time to see if one hears better than the other. Test children individually.

Activity 2: Make some ears from card
See if this helps hearing. Does directional or distance hearing improve?

Activity 3
Go outside on a windy day. In pairs the children can try shouting at each other from opposite ends of the playground or playing field. Also try this on a calm, still day. What effect does the wind have on the ability of the sound to travel?

Activity 4
Make a megaphone from thin card or paper and see if the children think it has any effect on the volume of sound or the ability to direct it.

This can also be used as an ear trumpet. Can the children hear better if they use this?

Activity 5
Doctors use a stethoscope to listen to sounds in our chests. Try to borrow one and try it out. If not, a useful substitute is a length of plastic tubing and two funnels.

Listen to the ticking of a watch using the tube. Does it sound louder than when one is standing the same distance away listening through the air?

Activity 6
The tube can also be used for speaking down. What does the voice sound like?

Activity 7
Sounds can travel quicker through some materials. Usually when we speak, the sound travels through air. Sea mammals such as whales and dolphins communicate underwater through sound. Their wide spectrum of sounds can carry over long distances, sometimes hundreds of miles. What is the longest distance the children's voices travelled outside? What other environmental sounds can the children hear outside? Is there a railway or a motorway nearby? A train can be heard approaching through the metal of the track long before the sound of the train reaches our ears through the air.

Try this test. Get a long piece of wood and a long piece of metal. Trying each in turn, put one end to the bone behind the ear and have one end touching the watch. Can the ticking of the watch be heard best at this distance through the air, through the wood or through the metal?

Activity 8

Make a telephone using two tin cans or two yoghurt pots. Thread string through holes in the bottom of the container. You can try different lengths of string to see what is the greatest distance at which it will operate. Start off with a two metre length. The string must be pulled tight. If one child speaks into one end the second may hear the voice at the other end, as the sound travels along the string. See whether the yoghurt pots or the cans make the best telephone.

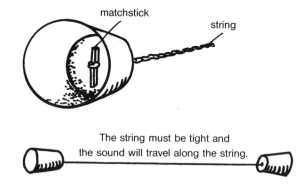

The string must be tight and the sound will travel along the string.

Copymasters

Use copymaster 71 (Picking up sounds) to measure how far away sounds can be heard with ear cups and without ear cups. Use a trundle wheel for long distances. You can also use the sheet to test how well the children can hear from different directions. Colour the appropriate box at the bottom of the sheet to indicate the direction the sound came from.

Area of study 3

MAKING SOUNDS

C72

Purpose

To show how musical sounds are produced by simple musical instruments.

Materials needed

A collection of different instruments: drums, woodwind, brass, tubular bells, strings (including violin, harp, guitar) and tuned and non-tuned percussion instruments.

Activity 1

Make a collection of as wide a range of instruments as possible and let the children experiment with making sound, at this stage in small groups if possible. As a class discuss how the various sounds were made and sort the instruments into sets accordingly. Was the instrument blown, struck, scraped, shaken or plucked? Is a piano plucked or struck to make the sound? Take the cover off and observe.

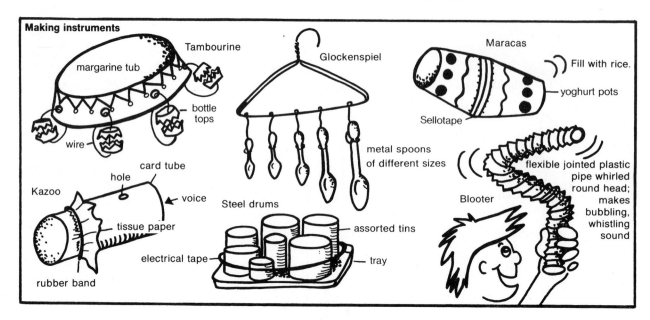

Making instruments

Activity 2

Test to see if the sounds or notes can be produced in more than one way, e.g. a tambourine can be beaten and shaken, a violin can be plucked or scraped with a bow and a harmonica will produce a sound if sucked or blown.

Activity 3

See if the children can see how the notes are changed on a tuned instrument such as a guitar and violin or what happens if the holes on woodwind instruments are covered or the valves on brass pressed when they are blown.

Activity 4

Make some instruments which are used in different ways to make sound.

Copymasters

Use copymaster 72 (Making sounds) to record how the note or sound was produced on the instrument shown, by writing the word for the action in the space below the picture.

Attainment target 15: Using light and electromagnetic radiation

Pupils should develop their knowledge and understanding of the properties and behaviour of light and electromagnetic waves.

Level 2	**Statements of attainment**

Pupils should:

- know that light passes through some materials and not others, and that when it does not, shadows may be formed.
- be able to draw pictures, showing features such as light, colour and shade.

 Area of study 1

LIGHT PASSES THROUGH THINGS

C73

Purpose

To show that light passes through some materials and not others.

Materials needed

A selection of torches of different sizes, a collection of different materials and articles (some of which are transparent, translucent and opaque) – include an assortment of plastic and glass bottles of different colours, different fabrics and papers, water, different oils and plastic sheeting.

Activity 1

Sort your collection of things using the torches as the light source. Let the children work in pairs, one shining the torch at the object while the other is on the opposite side to see if the light can be seen and to what extent. Ask them to classify the items using these criteria:

a) If they can see straight through the material clearly enough to see not only the torch light, but also the child holding the torch and all his/her features, then the material is transparent. You may want to class it as 'see-through'.
b) If they can see only the brightness of the light, but no distinct features and images appear blurred, then the material is translucent. You may wish to class it as 'almost see-through'. These materials let some of

the light through but the structure of the material scatters the light and gives an indistinct image.
c) If they cannot see through at all then this material is opaque and will not let any light through. You may wish to class it as 'can't see through'.

Make three sets of the objects: transparent, translucent and opaque.

You can record these findings on a check list:

Does light pass through this?			
material tested	see-through: transparent	almost see-through: translucent	can't see through: opaque
Cellophane			
woollen jumper			
book			
china cup			
pot cup			
tin can			
water			
oil			

Activity 2

You will need to help the children reach the general conclusion that we see things because light is present and if light is completely cut off from the object, then it cannot be seen. Put an object in a cardboard box and because the light is prevented from entering the box, the object is invisible. Put the same object in a transparent plastic box through which light can enter and the thing inside becomes visible. Look at the torches themselves. Does the light from the electric element go through the glass of the bulb and the glass of the torch face?

Activity 3

Try shining the torches through coloured plastic and glass bottles, and coloured Cellophane. Light goes through them, but if you look through them, the things you are looking at seem to change colour. It is not necessary at this stage to talk about the spectrum (see Level 3) but in fact the coloured transparent material acts as a colour filter, only allowing light of its own colour to pass through.

Have a disco! Cover the ends of the torches with pieces of different coloured Cellophane, using a rubber band to secure them. Find a dark place and a 'ghetto blaster' for your music and have the torches flashed as you dance.

Activity 4: Try different liquids

Having established that clear plastic bottles are transparent, fill several with the following and test for transparency by shining a torch through the bottle: milk, clean tap water, dirty water, soapy water, muddy water, cooking oil, clean car oil, dirty car oil, jelly, etc.

Activity 5

Try different fabrics and papers and see if you can find examples of all three types: transparent, translucent and opaque. Try to ally the transparency of the material to its use, for example, tracing paper needs to be sturdy and see-through, Cellophane is used in cases when light needs to be seen clearly.

Activity 6: Make a glass display

Some bottle banks confuse adults by labelling glass brown, green and clear. Of course all bottles are clear and the third should read 'colourless'. Try to collect as many single examples of different colours of bottles or other glass items as possible.

Copymasters

Use copymaster 73 (Now you see it, now you don't) to record the initial classification into three sets: transparent, translucent and opaque.

Area of study 2

SHADOWS

C74

Purpose

To show that when light cannot pass through a material, shadows may be formed.

Materials needed

Slide projector, selection of torches, paper, pens, plastic straws, scissors, Sellotape.

Activity 1: Make shadows

Objects which do not let light through cast a shadow which is the place where light from the light source cannot reach. The light lands on the surface (floor, wall etc.) all around the object. Experiment with a variety of small objects and a torch. Turn the objects in

different directions and shine the torch on them from different directions. Observe the different shaped shadows which can be seen by moving one object.

Activity 2: Giant shadows

Many children will already know the fun of playing with shadows on a sunny day, so recreate this in the school hall with the slide projector. Simply shine the beam on the biggest wall and see who can make the biggest and most fearsome shadow monster on the wall. Get the children to use their whole bodies. Experiment with standing near to and far from the projector beam. Does it make the shadow larger or smaller, distinct or fuzzy? Talk about what shadows look like.

Changing shadows

Move objects to change
the size of the shadow.

Activity 3

Go outside on a sunny day and experiment on the playground. Use PE equipment to create illusions. Make tall shadows, tiny shadows and funny shapes. Jump on your shadow or on a friend's shadow's head. Working with a friend, try to make your shadows shake hands without actually touching hands. Try moving without your shadow moving . . . it can be done!

'Go outside and play.'

Draw a friend.

Make a small shadow.

Make a tall shadow.

Make funny shapes.

Hold things.

Touch your own shadow and try to catch a friend's shadow. Play with bubbles. Do they make shadows? Do you get shadows on a cloudy day? Discuss the way an object's shadow moves and changes shape as the Sun moves in the sky.

Activity 4

Make shadow puppets, using hands or card cut-outs.

Activity 5

Plot the movement of the Sun during the day. The Sun as a major light source is the cause of most shadows. Stick a paper marker on the sunniest window in the classroom and mark the progress of its shadow during the day, as shown.

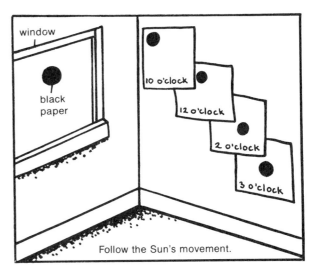

window

black paper

10 o'clock

12 o'clock

2 o'clock

3 o'clock

Follow the Sun's movement.

Activity 6: Make silhouette pictures

Using a slide projector as the light source let children draw round a friend's shadow on the wall. Stick white paper on the wall, draw round the shadow with pencil and fill in with black paint, cut out and mount on a variety of colours.

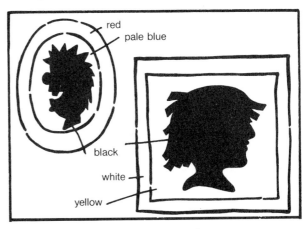

red

pale blue

black

white

yellow

Copymasters

Use copymaster 74 (Shadows) to record how the shadow cast by an object changes shape depending on the direction of the light source. In each of the three examples the children are to draw where the shadow of the cup will fall and its shape.

85

DRWING

C75

Purpose
To show children how to draw, showing features such as light, colour and shade.

Materials needed
Paints, papers, felt pens, pencils, anglepoise lamp or torches.

Activity 1
In order to see the effect of light upon colour and shade it will be necessary to give a great deal of practice in observation of the effect as well as in actual drawing from direct observation.

Using the natural light first and some simple shaped objects such as a teddy, a ball, a box, a vase, a cardboard tube, place each on a table and discuss how the colour of the objects seems to change depending on how the light strikes them: looking darker on the side away from the light and vice versa.

Observe how the objects also cast a shadow on the side which is away from the light source.

Draw a selection of these simple shaped things, using pencil. Get the children to draw the object first and then to show you where they can see shade on the object itself and finally to point out where this shading should be on their picture. You can then show them how to shade the picture using their pencils. Last of all draw in any shadows the object casts. Use an artificial light source as well.

Encourage the children to draw only what they see and not what they think they should see, e.g. if the handle of a cup is not visible from their point of view, then they should not draw it in.

Activity 2
Obtain some decorators' colour charts and cut up one colour shade strip, e.g. the reds. Cut up the strip into its several shades and ask the children to order these from palest to darkest. Let them work in pairs or small groups so that they can discuss their ideas. Talk about the names given to these different shades, e.g. magenta, cerise, blood red, rose, blush, etc.

Activity 3: Mix paint
Using only black and white and starting with white, add a little black at a time to make as many shades of grey as possible. As you add a little more black, paint one stripe of the new shade each time.

Activity 4
Use coloured paints and experiment with white added to each colour to produce a range of shades as in the paints charts. Make up names for each of your new shades such as, 'rain cloud blue, laurel green, tarmac grey, cement grey, bark red, fried egg yellow, stew brown, baby milk white'.

Make a paint chart of your own, using your own names for each shade. Do the same sort of thing adding black, but be careful to add the black to the colour a little at a time and not the other way round, as you will need a great deal of paint to have any effect on black.

Activity 5: Draw using colour
Collect a range of small things which have different colours in them and encourage the children to draw them, trying to match the exact colour of the object with their felt pens or coloured pencils. Both of these media can be mixed to obtain different shades.

Encourage the children to observe how the colours change shade depending on how much light falls on them.

Copymasters
Use copymaster 75 (Shades and shadows) to record this Area of Study. The children have to draw the Sun anywhere they like in the sky. Remember that the Sun can go as low as the horizon line shown. The children must next colour the picture and finally add shading and shadows depending on the position of the Sun. You can use this sheet several times and put the Sun in a different position each time.

Attainment target 16: The Earth in space

Pupils should develop their knowledge and understanding of the relative positions and movement of the Earth, Moon, Sun and solar system within the universe.

| Level 2 | **Statements of attainment** |

Pupils should:

- be able to explain why night occurs.
- know that day length changes throughout the year.
- know that we live on a large, spherical, self-contained planet, called Earth.
- know that the Earth, Moon and Sun are separate bodies.

THE SUN, THE MOON, THE STARS

 C76

Purpose
To show that the Earth, Moon and Sun are separate bodies and that we live on Earth.

Materials needed
Space charts, posters, videos, Earth globe, Moon globe, satellite photographs, tubes, boxes, cartons, glue, scissors, card, felt pens.

Activity 1
Write to NASA and get as much information as possible about the American space programme. Make a display of the photographs and posters and any toy or model space rockets, shuttles and space machines the children are able to bring in. There is quite a lot of video material now available of the Earth from outer space which shows that the Earth is a large, spherical, self-contained planet.

Activity 2
Use the globe to show the shape of the Earth and the various points of interest on it such as the North Pole, South Pole, the British Isles, the major continents: Africa, the Americas, Australia, Asia and Europe.

Activity 3
Look at satellite pictures used in weather forecasts. Talk about how these help to predict the weather.

Activity 4
Look at charts of the solar system and look at the positions of the Sun and planets. Point out the Earth and the Moon. There are Moon globes available which show the positions of the seas and craters. Ask the children to look at the full Moon at night to see if they can spot any of these larger features. A fairly low-power telescope will make a significant difference when looking for details in the night sky.

Activity 5
Make model rockets, space vehicles and satellites. Children can design their own moon buggy. Try to incorporate as many aspects of CDT in this activity as possible.

Copymasters
Use copymaster 76 (The Sun, Moon and Earth) to reinforce the facts that the Sun is a star, the Earth is a planet that goes round it and the Moon goes round the Earth. Discuss the illustration and point out that it is merely to show the fact that the three things are all separate. Refer the children to the picture of the solar system to show the Earth's position relative to the Sun and the other planets.

NIGHT

C77

Purpose
To explain why night occurs.

Materials needed
Globe, torch, matchstick, Sellotape.

Activity 1
Follow up the work from Level 1 about observation of the Sun in the sky and its apparent movement across it (see page 34). Go out in the late afternoon of the autumn term and look at the position of the Sun on the horizon. Children can observe the Sun setting and the onset of darkness and night.

Activity 2
In school the next day you can demonstrate how the Earth moves on its axis to produce night. Look at the globe with the children and mark on it the countries

they have visited and the one where they live. Mark them with a matchstick Sellotaped in place. Go into a darkened room and shine the torch, representing the Sun, on to the globe on the side where the British Isles are. Turn the globe slowly to imitate the movement of the Earth and watch how the different parts of the 'Earth' are in 'daytime' or 'night-time'. Ask the children to watch for the 'time change' in the places they marked. To show that the Earth spins on its own axis as it also journeys round the Sun, have one child carrying the turning globe as he/she walks round a child holding a large beach ball which represents the Sun.

Copymasters
Use copymaster 77 (Why night occurs) to record this activity. The children are given a structure within which to write a record of what they did and observed.

Blu-Tack® or Sellotape   matchstick

 Area of study 3

DAY LENGTH

 C78

Purpose
To show that day length changes throughout the year.

Materials needed
Pictures of outdoors (day and night), children playing in day or at night, clothes with reflective strips on.

Activity 1
The spring or autumn terms are the best times to observe changes in day length.

Start at the beginning of the terms and record twice a week the times it went dark. A simple chart like this can be taken home by the children and the date and time recorded.

What time does it go dark ?	
date	it went dark at:
September 24th.	6.05 p.m.
September 28th.	5.55 p.m.
October 1st.	5.48 p.m.
October 5th.	5.38 p.m.
October 8th.	5.31 p.m.
October 12th.	5.22 p.m.

The observations can be taken over the months of September, October, November and December. At the end of the term it will be topical to talk about how the children now go home in the dark. You can note the time it becomes light in the morning and the time it goes dark and work out the day length. Days are now much shorter.

Activity 2
Talk about safety in the dark, particularly road safety and the need to wear something light at night. Reflective strips can be bought for children's clothing. Try to collect other items of 'day-glow' clothing which night workers such as the emergency services wear.

Talk about going home from school in the summer term when it is often sunny and warm.

Activity 3
Discuss after-school activities which have a direct relation to the length of day. Summer term after-school activities may well be outdoor ones such as riding a bike or playing in the park, garden or paddling pool. Contrast these activities with winter ones which may be indoor: watching television, reading, playing with computer games and so on.

Do a survey of favourite summer activities and winter ones. You could do a survey to find out what is the most popular parental curfew time in the summer.

Copymasters
Use copymaster 78 (After school) to show the different appearance of the same time of day at two different times of year, e.g. winter and summer after school.

Children draw themselves and their friends going home from school. They should draw lights from houses and vehicles, the Sun or the Moon and light or dark sky as the case may be. Remember to discuss the sort of clothes they would be wearing at the different times of the year, depending on the weather.

LEVEL 3

Attainment target 1: Exploration of science

Pupils should develop the intellectual and practical skills that allow them to explore the world of science and to develop a fuller understanding of scientific phenomena and the procedures of scientific exploration and investigation. This work should take place in the context of activities that require a progressively more systematic and quantified approach, which draws upon an increasing knowledge and understanding of science. The activities should encourage the ability to:

i. plan, hypothesise and predict
ii. design and carry out investigations
iii. interpret results and findings
iv. draw inferences
v. communicate exploratory tasks and experiments.

Level 3

Statements of attainment

Pupils should:

- formulate hypotheses, for example, *'this ball will bounce higher than that one'*.
- identify, and describe simple variables that change over time, for example, *growth of a plant*.
- distinguish between a 'fair' and an 'unfair' test.
- select and use simple instruments to enhance observations, for example, *a stop-clock or hand lens*.
- quantify variables, as appropriate, to the nearest labelled division of simple measuring instruments, for example, *a rule*.
- record experimental findings, for example, *in tables and bar charts*.
- interpret simple pictograms and bar charts.
- interpret observations in terms of a generalised statement, for example, *the greater the suspended weight, the longer the spring*.
- describe activities carried out by sequencing the major features.

As the children are working on the activities at this level they will have the opportunity to do work contributing to AT1 as the activities in the text are all designed to do this.

For example in AT11 (Electricity and magnetism), Area of Study 1, Activity 3, the children are asked to test several designs for electrical circuits, and in doing so will be satisfying the requirements of AT1 by identifying differences in the circuits, formulating hypotheses about which they think should work,

designing tests to find out which work by looking at the order of elements in the circuit and finally by recording their findings on the copymaster.

A bar code of symbols relating to AT1 has been created. Below is the key to it.

The full bar code appears on the record sheet to help you record the children's experiences. These symbols, which are linked to work on the copymasters, appear in the text at the appropriate place.

Observation

Discussion

Formulate
hypotheses

Identify

Fair/unfair
test

Use
instruments

Quantify
variables

Record

Interpret
charts

Interpret and
generalise

Sequencing

Attainment target 2: The variety of life

Pupils should develop their knowledge and understanding of the diversity and classification of past and present life-forms, and of the relationships, energy flows, cycles of matter and human influences within ecosystems.

Level
3

Statements of attainment

Pupils should:

- be able to recognise similarities and differences among living things.
- be able to sort living things into broad groups according to observable features.
- know that living things respond to seasonal and daily changes.

Area of study 1

CHANGES

C79

Purpose
To show that living things respond to seasonal and daily changes.

Materials needed
Pictures and photographs of plants and animals during the day and at night, during different seasons; ice plants, runner beans, dandelions, seed catalogues and gardening brochures.

Activity 1: Looking at plants
It is easiest to look at the two main categories of living things, plants and animals (including humans) separately in order to try to find out how they respond to seasonal changes.

Plants need heat, light and water. Certain plants such as ice plants (mesembryanthemums) respond very quickly to light. Grow them in pots and watch them close their petals when put in the shade and re-open when in full sunlight. Dandelions close their flowers at dusk. Observe the way plants droop in hot sunshine and revive when they are watered and put in the shade for a period.

Point out that plants need warmth; an overnight frost can damage or kill young plants and a previously healthy plant can be changed dramatically. Also, plants will only thrive when all the conditions are right and certain plants have a growing season.

During the year the children can observe and record the planting of seeds, the germination and growth, the flowering and dying of easily grown annuals such as Virginia stock. Try growing them in winter. Sow the seeds outdoors and indoors to see which germinate.

Activity 2: Looking at trees
Look at the way trees change through the seasons.

Activity 3: Looking at flowers
Sort flowers into spring, summer, autumn and winter blooms, using seed and gardening catalogues to provide pictures for sorting into the groups. Does the temperature affect the growth of seedlings?

Activity 4: Growing seedlings
Three trays of seedlings are required. They are placed in three places with very different temperatures: the oven (very low temperature), the freezer and the classroom. Show the children the different temperatures on the thermometer; they will of course instinctively appreciate the temperature differences. Discuss the variable of time and how long the seedlings should be left in each place.

Discuss with the children the factors that will make this a fair test:

a) The growing medium should be the same and of the same depth.
b) Seedlings should be of the same age and size.
c) There should be a light source.
d) The seedlings should be in the same type and size of shallow metal or earthenware container.
e) The seedlings should have been watered regularly with the same amount of water before the test commences.
f) The duration of the experiment should be decided.
g) Observe the results and record pictorially or use Copymaster 79 for this purpose.

Activity 5: Looking at animals
If possible look at pets and observe how they respond to changes such as a new cage, or new food. What do they do on a hot or a cold day?

Most wild animals have their young in the spring when the extremes of winter are more likely to be over. The young have a better chance of survival when the days are longer and warmer and food more plentiful. Look for examples of animals responding to seasonal changes: birds building nests, frog spawn, the presence of more insects, lambs, ducklings, etc. In the autumn and winter we can look for different responses to the changing seasons such as birds getting ready to migrate, frogs and hedgehogs hibernating and squirrels gathering nuts.

Activity 6: Looking at ourselves
We need food daily and if we miss a meal we feel hungry; if we do not get enough sleep we feel tired and

90

if we do not get enough to drink we are thirsty. The children may like to try going without their mid-morning snack or drink to see what temporary hunger is like.

We respond to the weather on a daily basis by wearing suitable clothes. The children can identify the type of clothes they need for different types of weather. Also, the weather may affect our emotions: sunny weather can make us feel cheerful, but we are disappointed if the bad weather forces us to cancel a special event or an outing. Make lists of the different hobbies, activities, festivals and holidays which are common to different seasons.

Copymasters
Use copymaster 79 (Changes) to record the effect of one possible change on seedlings. The children are to draw the seedlings in each situation and write a short piece on what happened.

 Area of study 2

SIMILARITIES AND DIFFERENCES

Purpose
To be able to recognise similarities and differences among living things.

Outline activities
a) Look at the way living things move, whether they walk on two or four legs, crawl, swim or fly.
b) Look at the shape of the face, position of eyes and ears, nose and mouth.
c) Look at coverings: skin, fur, hair, feathers, scales.
d) Find out what they eat: meat, vegetation or both.
e) Make lists of animals which: fly, swim, live in caves, build nests, eat meat, eat plants.
f) Make lists of plants which: grow in woods, in deserts, have flowers, have woody stems, have broad flat leaves, etc.

When the lists are complete see if some creatures appear in more than one list.

 Area of study 3

SORTING LIVING THINGS

Purpose
To sort living things into broad groups according to observable features.

Outline activities
List the observable features of different groups of animals:

Birds	Fish	Mammals	Reptiles
feathers	scales	hair or fur	skin
beaks	teeth	teeth	teeth
noses	gills	noses	noses
wings	fins	legs	legs
fly/walk/ swim	swim	swim/walk/ climb	swim/walk/ climb
lay eggs	lay eggs	live young feed milk	lay eggs

Sort out the selection of animals into different groups according to observable features so that a child can look at a picture, the animal or a video and say, 'This animal is covered in feathers, it builds nests, lays eggs, has a beak. It is a bird.'

Attainment target 3: Processes of life

Pupils should develop their knowledge and understanding of the organisation of living things and of the processes which characterise their survival and reproduction.

Level
3

Statements of attainment

Pupils should:

- know that the basic life processes: feeding, breathing, movement and behaviour, are common to human beings and the other living things they have studied.
- be able to describe the main stages in the human life cycle.

Area of study 1

LIFE PROCESSES

C80

Purpose
To show that the life processes are common to all living things.

Materials needed
Set of toy farm and zoo animals, photographs of a wide variety of animals showing movement, social behaviour, feeding, wildlife videos.

Activity 1: How animals feed
Start with the children and talk about the kinds of foods we eat which are in the main categories of meat, vegetables, fruit and so on. Discuss ethnic differences in diet and even try out some foods from other cultures. This experience can be linked with the section on behaviour. Illustrate this with pictures of different meals (see below).

Human beings are omnivorous. They can eat both meat and vegetables. Although some people opt for a vegetarian diet the human constitution allows us to eat both, whereas some animals are adapted for digesting one or the other.

Watch selections of wildlife videos showing a variety of animals feeding. All animals can be divided according to their feeding habits. They are either carnivorous (meat eating), herbivorous (plant eating) or omnivorous (eating both meat and plants).

Using the toy zoo and farm animals, talk about the animals seen on the video and sort the toys into three sets according to their feeding habits. Carnivorous animals generally kill certain other species of animal for food, but sometimes eat only dead animals. The herbivorous animals spend their time fleeing from predators. Omnivores do both. In each case the feeding habits dictate a large part of the animals' behaviour.

Activity 2: How plants feed
Using the simple experiments described on pages 36 and 37, deprive plants of: a) water b) light c) soil and see if they grow well. Discuss how to make the tests fair. You will need to have a supply of control plants. Record observations. Plants take in nutrients from the soil through their roots, along the stems to their leaves. Watch this by putting coloured ink in water and standing a white carnation in the water. It will slowly take on the colour of the ink.

Activity 3: How animals breathe

Watch a variety of animals breathing. You may be able to bring pets into school for the children to observe.

Remember DES and LEA regulations on animals in school and RSPCA guidelines on animals' welfare.

Try to observe fish, small and large mammals, birds, reptiles and amphibians. It is difficult to observe breathing in animals such as insects but you may get close-up material on wildlife videos. Watch how humans breathe first and measure the breathing rate of the children before and after the exercise. Encourage the children to guess first and then test their hypothesis. At this stage they can begin to work out their own tests.

Try to work out how to measure the breathing rate of any animals you may be able to observe at first hand. Smaller animals have a faster breathing rate. You may be able to visit a zoo and watch a large animal such as an elephant breathing. Try to find out how animals such as amphibians, sponges and worms breathe. You will need to find out about the animals which breathe with gills instead of lungs.

Activity 4: How plants breathe

Plants exchange gases during the process of photosynthesis, giving out oxygen and taking in carbon dioxide. A bottle garden will show how plants give out

water vapour and re-use that water in the constant exchange which creates our air.

Activity 3: Animal movement

Watch wildlife videos or go to the zoo or a farm and observe a variety of animals moving. Make lists of the different movers, e.g. animals which: run or walk, gallop, leap and hop, fly, swim, slide, crawl, climb. Look for special adaptations which suit the animal for its purpose or the habitat in which it lives, such as claws for digging or climbing, hooves for galloping, wings, flippers, fins and so on. Look at pictures of a variety of limbs and try to work out what they are used for, then watch video material to find out.

Activity 5: Plant movement

Plant movement is so slow it is difficult to observe. However, plants which are insectivorous like the Venus fly trap can be seen to move with the naked eye if they are fed! Videos of time lapse photography showing plant movement would be invaluable and the BBC may be able to help obtain such material. Try putting pots of young, tender plants of a taller variety in different positions around the classroom and watch how the plants bend towards the light.

Activity 6: Animal behaviour

Again wildlife videos will be invaluable. Look at feeding habits, try to observe whether the animal is a predator or preyed upon. Look at social behaviour,

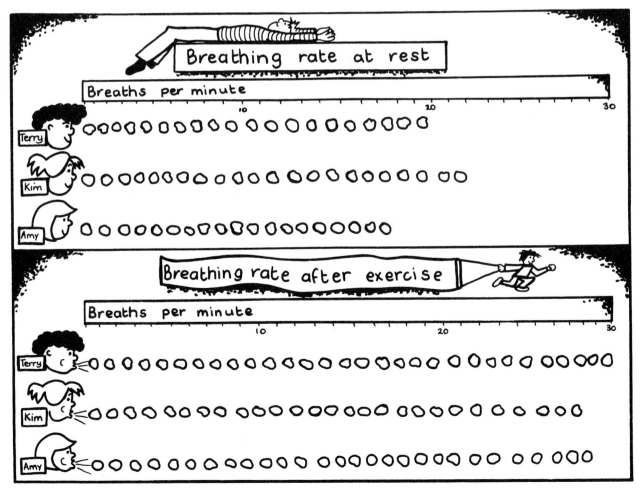

using videos, reference books and first hand observation where possible to find out whether animals are gregarious and if so what sort of groups they live in. Try to find out about territorial behaviour, courtship rituals, family life, whether the mother takes care of the young, how these young learn to be adults and hierarchies within a group. Find out how the animals communicate successfully within the species and with man, using several animals (dogs are a good example).

Discuss the kind of emotions which the children's pets show. How do we know what they are?

Activity 7: Plant behaviour
Look at how plants are adapted to different conditions such as cold, heat, water, wind. Some people think plants communicate like animals. Try talking to some classroom plants and not others to see if they respond. Look at how plants congregate; do they grow in huge groups or solitarily? How do they reproduce?

Copymasters
Use copymaster 80 (What is it?) to record this Area of Study. The children draw an animal in the top box and then having found out about it from observation or research they write in detail about its life style and life processes.

 HUMAN LIFE CYCLE

Purpose
To study the main stages in the human life cycle.

Outline activities
a) Talk about the children's own lives so far. Collect photographs of them at various stages of development, one per year since birth.

b) Talk about pregnancy and birth, the developmental and social milestones in their lives, getting married, families, old age. Invite old people into school to talk and help out. Look at the skills of children who are younger and older.

c) Make a diary of life so far: 'When I was one I could . . .'

Attainment target 4: Genetics and evolution

Pupils should develop their knowledge and understanding of variation and its genetic and environmental causes and the basic mechanisms of inheritance, selection and evolution.

Level 3	**Statements of attainment**

Pupils should:

● know that some life forms became extinct a long time ago and others more recently.

 PREHISTORIC LIFE

Purpose
To be able to identify the evidence of extinct life forms and a range of dinosaurs.

Materials needed
Collection of fossil plants and animals, pictures, posters and books about dinosaurs, model dinosaurs, card, plaster of Paris, Plasticine®, shoe polish.

Activity 1
Collect together photographs, pictures and books about prehistoric life. Some of the children will have toy models of Tyrannosaurus Rex, Brontosaurus and Stegosaurus which they can bring in.

Let the children look at the photographs, books and models and talk about the variety of creatures: those which walked on four legs or two, the flying dinosaurs and the huge lumbering vegetarian dinosaurs. Compare present day large animals such as the elephant with the dinosaurs to give an idea of size. Talk about why the creatures died out and point out that despite certain cinema films, humans did not live on Earth at the same time as dinosaurs.

Activity 2
If there is an area where fossils are to be found in your neighbourhood, take the children out to hunt for them. Common places are quarries, mines and areas of limestone pavement.

Obviously, precipitous locations are not suitable.

Some LEAs have a museum loans service which may lend fossil material, depending on the local area. Nearby secondary schools may be prepared to lend their collection if they have one.

If possible let the children handle the fossils to get an idea of texture, weight, shape and the experience of handling something far older than themselves (or even their teacher!). Talk about how fossils are made and look at coal.

Activity 3
Set up a diorama to show off the various dinosaur models and let the children draw from the models.

Activity 4: Model fossils
The children can make plaster casts of some common fossils, ammonites, trilobites, ferns, footprints and shells.

The method is as follows:

a) Make an impression of a fern in Plasticine®.
b) Place the Plasticine® impression on the bottom of a shallow tray or box.
c) Pour plaster over the top of the Plasticine®.

d) When set, peel off the Plasticine®. There will be a raised impression of the fern.
e) Brush with shoe polish and shine with a soft cloth.

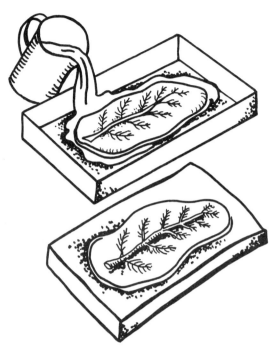

Place alongside real fossils on the display.

Copymasters
Use copymaster 81 (Prehistoric life) and the books, pictures and models to find out as much as possible about the different kinds of dinosaurs as listed on the sheet. The children can draw their own picture in the box and then write about it in the space provided.

 ANIMALS IN DANGER ▶

Area of study 2

Purpose
To identify those creatures which have become extinct or are threatened with extinction.

Outline activities
a) Get pictures of the dodo and the moa and other creatures which have recently become extinct and talk about the factors that caused them to disappear. The dodo was hunted for food and the eggs were taken too.
b) Talk about man's other destructive influences, e.g. the destruction of an animal's natural habitat, the introduction of non-native animals which are predatory or which eat the same food as native ones. Pollution has caused disease in some creatures and many thousands have died as a result.
c) Find out about the animals currently in danger such as the African elephant, the white rhino, the giant panda, the whale and even the humble badger in Britain. Organisations such as Greenpeace or the World Wide Fund for Nature will give lots of information on the plight of these animals. Children might discuss ways in which they can help save some of these creatures. Once they become extinct they are gone forever and the only record of their existence will be in photographs or on film.

Attainment target 5: Human influences on the Earth

Pupils should develop their knowledge and understanding of the ways in which human activities affect the Earth.

Level 3

Statements of attainment

Pupils should:

- know that human activity may produce local changes in the Earth's surface, air and water.
- be able to give an account of a project to help improve the local environment.

 Area of study 1

HUMAN ACTIVITY AND CHANGES C82

Purpose
To show that human activity may produce changes in the Earth's surface, air or water.

Materials needed
Globe of the world, nature videos of different parts of the world, junk materials for model making, glue, scissors, pens.

Activity 1
Watch video material of lands which have little or no human influence on the environment, e.g. polar regions, the large deserts, jungles and forests, the oceans, the prairies. There are very few untouched areas of the world now! Identify these places on a globe.

Activity 2
Talk about the neighbourhood round school and make a list of all the human activities which are going on. It will be difficult for children to understand that humans have made 'natural looking' farmland.

Activity 3
Go for a walk around the neighbourhood looking for man-made features such as quarries, reservoirs, parkland. Try to get a sense of position, e.g. the school is next to a main road and across the road are other houses.

Activity 4
Study large-scale maps of your area and try to identify the man-made features such as roads, canals, conurbations, parks, forested areas, reservoirs. Make a separate search for features such as rivers, mountains and sea.

Activity 5
Make a 3D map of your area including as many man-made and natural features as possible. Mark the features which are man-made with a red flag.

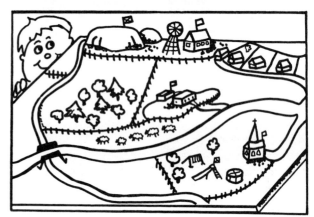

Activity 6
Draw a pictorial map of the area. The important thing is to include features whose relationship to each other can be described, e.g. the school is in-between a coal mine and a farm and there is a motorway at the end of the road. Scale is unimportant at this stage.

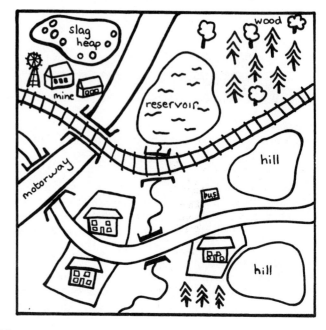

96

Activity 7
Discuss the effects of the features observed in Activity 6. Make lists of good things, e.g. lovely green fields on the farms, beautiful trees in the forest and park, power from electricity, etc., and the bad, such as noise, air and water pollution, crowding of roads, chemicals in the soil, erosion of soil due to hedges being pulled up, waste blowing from tips.

Copymasters
Use copymaster 82 (Our neighbourhood) to record this Area of Study. The children can write a short commentary on which human activities have affected their area and how.

 LOCAL PROJECT ▶

Purpose
To give an account of a local project to help the environment.

Outline activities
Projects could include pond clearance, tree planting, clearance of waste ground, planting wind breaks, fencing, pathmaking, making crossings for animals, painting out graffiti.

Children can record the project with drawings and paintings, photograph and video and on tape recorder. It is essential to record what the area looked like before the project started, while the work is in progress and of course, when it is completed. Much discussion will be involved at the planning stage, when the order of jobs and materials needed is decided.

Attainment target 6: Types and uses of materials

Pupils should develop their knowledge and understanding of the properties of materials and the way properties of materials determine their uses and form the basis for their classification.

Level 3

Statements of attainment

Pupils should:

- know that some materials occur naturally while many are made from raw materials.
- be able to list the similarities and differences in a variety of everyday materials.

 SIMILARITIES AND DIFFERENCES ▶

Purpose
To be able to list similarities and differences in a range of everyday materials.

Materials needed
Samples of: cotton, wool, different fabrics, leather, rubber, iron, steel, brass, bronze, copper, precious metal (if available!), cement, stone, clay, brick, sand, wood, coal, plastic, polystyrene, glass, paper, cardboard, water, lemonade, custard, jelly, air.

Activity 1: Qualities of materials
Let the children look at and examine all the materials and discuss their obvious qualities, e.g. their colour, texture and state, i.e. solid, liquid or gas. It will be fairly easy to sort the materials into these three sets. One

problem may be how to contain the air in order to sort it! See AT9 Level 3 (page 100) for suggestions.

Activity 2: Changes of state
Discuss the notion of an object changing its state. For example, when does custard stop being a liquid and become a solid? Make some and see. What are the characteristics of a solid? It could be described as a material that can maintain a shape of its own, e.g. custard set in a mould shape. See AT6 Level 2 (pages 54–6) for work on changes of state.

A liquid needs to be kept in a vessel and cannot keep a shape of its own. If it is released from a vessel it will break up and find its way to the lowest possible point, e.g. water always runs downhill. Demonstrate this by spilling some water on to soil and watching it soak down through the soil.

A gas hangs in the 'air' at different levels depending on its density. Generally speaking gases cannot be held and are usually invisible, but can be caught in a vessel such as a balloon! Catch some air in a plastic bag by billowing out the bag and holding the neck closed when it is inflated.

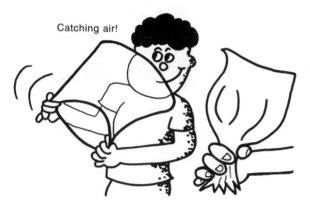

Catching air!

Activity 3: Flexibility

Try bending a material. Does it bend and remain bent or does it spring back or move back to the original position slowly? Does it bend only so far and then break? Does it bend when warm or wet but break when cold and dry? You could make a holding point, for example, a large bulldog clip nailed to a piece of wood wedged between two cupboards. Fix the material in this device and measure how far from the starting point the material will bend before it breaks or resists. Discuss why the children may not be able to bend a material further. Can someone stronger bend it further? Does the bulldog clip or the cupboard move when pushed by the material? Will you need to have all the materials in the same shape for this test, i.e. long strips?

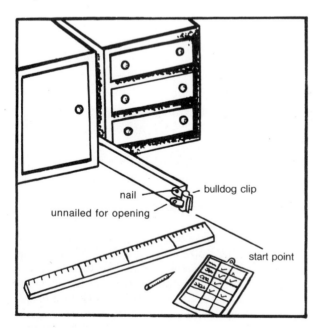

nail
bulldog clip
unnailed for opening
start point

Activity 4: Strength

Strength is allied to flexibility. Use weights to test the strengths of different materials resting on two supports. Will materials need to be the same length? Record the different breaking points of materials.

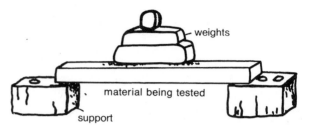

weights
material being tested
support

Fabrics and other non-rigid materials can be tested for strength by holding weights in them as in a hammock to see if they tear or disintegrate. Use same size pieces of material and record which broke at which weight from the least to the greatest. Start with the smallest weight and increase weight by 100 g at a time. For stronger materials you will need to be the hammock holder.

Activity 5: Stretch

Stretch is also allied to flexibility and strength. Test to see if a material can be made longer or wider by pulling. Some materials have so much elasticity that they will also return to their previous shape and size after stretching. Test by hand and then put them in order of stretchability.

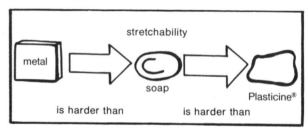

stretchability
metal
soap
Plasticine®
is harder than   is harder than

Activity 6: Hardness

Can you make a mark on one material with another? Children can test this and place the materials in order of hardness.

Activity 7: Transparency

Can you see a clear image through the material? Does it let light through but only as an indistinct, blurred image? Does it let no light through and cast a shadow itself?

Activity 8: Smell

Does the material have a smell and what emotion does this generate? Is it nice, tickly, awful, sweet? Is it like the smell of another material, e.g. a woody smell, a fatty smell, the smell of rotten eggs?

By looking at each of the properties in turn with a range of different materials the children can begin to recognise similarities and differences between materials.

Copymasters

Use copymaster 83 (Comparing materials) to record this Area of Study. Stick a small sample of the two materials in the space on the sheet and list the similarities in the central column and the differences in the outer columns.

Area of study 2

NATURAL OR MAN-MADE

Purpose
To be able to sort materials into two categories, naturally occurring and man-made.

Outline activities
A great deal of the information about natural and man-made materials will be received at second hand but there will be opportunities to develop research skills such as reading, writing for information, questioning people, etc. Make a collection of raw and man-made materials and identify them, then look at everyday objects and try to match materials to objects. Find sources of natural materials, such as wood, clay and stone and find out about manufacturing processes. Make displays to illustrate.

Attainment target 9: Earth and atmosphere

Pupils should develop their knowledge and understanding of the structure and main features of the Earth, the atmosphere and their changes over time.

Level 3

Statements of attainment

Pupils should:

- be able to describe from their observations some of the effects of weathering on buildings and on the landscape.
- know that air is all around us.
- understand how weathering of rocks leads to the formation of different types of soil.
- be able to give an account of an investigation of some natural material (rock or soil).
- be able to understand and interpret common meteorological symbols as used in the media.

 Area of study 1

AIR

 C84

Purpose
To show that air is all around us.

Materials needed
Large sheet of cardboard, jam jar and candle, art straw, wool, two balloons, glass bottle with screw top, straw, Plasticine®, water (hot and cold), bowl, ping-pong ball.

Activity 1
Take a large piece of cardboard and wave it up and down to move the air. You could also make small individual fans. Take it in turns to make a wind in the classroom and see who can make a hurricane. You can look for other evidence of moving air: washing waving on the line, leaves blown in the wind, kites flying, trees bending.

Activity 2: Catch some air!

Blow up lots of balloons and play with them in the hall or outside. Ask the children to play with balloons in the bath to see if they can keep the air under water. They may already know that blow-up toys will float.

Ask the children how the air got into the balloons. Talk about breathing. Have a go at breathing!

Activity 3

Think of things that we use which are filled with air, either to bear weight, float or trap air to be used. Your list may contain tyres, balls, balloons, hot air balloons, inflatable dinghy, bouncy castles, swimming rings and arm bands, soap bubbles and breathing apparatus. Collect some of these things so that the children can examine some and use them.

Activity 4: Air is heavy

Take two inflated balloons and fix them to a simple balance as shown. Make them balance by moving the pivot. Now pop one balloon and see what happens.

Activity 5: Fire needs air

Light a candle and place a jam jar over it. When all the air inside the jar has been used up the flame will be extinguished. Even though the children cannot see the air they can see a result when air is trapped inside a small space and used.

Activity 6: Play with hot air!

Hot air expands and the results of this expansion can be seen quite clearly. Put a dent in a ping-pong ball and then float it in a bowl of hot water. The air inside the ball expands and pushes out the dent.

Any experiments involving hot water or fire must be closely supervised by the teacher.

Activity 7: Air changes size

Air expands and contracts. Using a glass bottle which will stand easily on its own, fill it with hot water to warm the glass, empty out two thirds of the water and quickly put a balloon over the bottle neck. It should pop up as it fills with the expanded warm air from the bottle. Now stand this bottle and balloon in a bowl of very cold water and as the air inside the bottle contracts the balloon will be sucked downwards into the neck of the bottle.

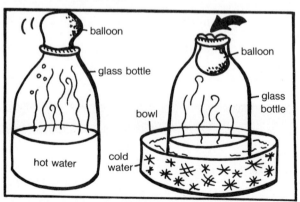

Activity 8: Make a fountain using hot air as power!

Set up the apparatus as shown at the top of page 101, half filling the bottle with cold water and standing it in a bowl of very hot water. As the air in the bottle is heated up by the water it expands and pushes down on the surface of the water, forcing the water out of the top of the straw.

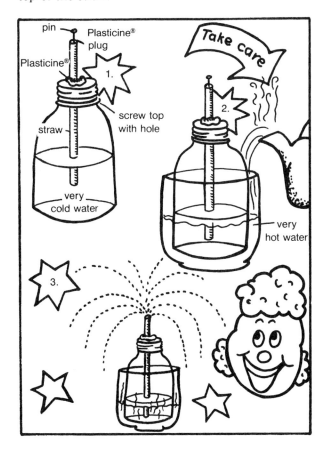

Activity 9: Make bubble prints
Put a little washing-up liquid into mixed powder paint and blow into the mixture with a straw until you have a fine head of bubbles. Place a sheet of paper over the bubbles which will leave a print of their outline. You can use several colours to make a design. Ask the children to think about breathing in before they blow so that they realise they are using air all around them.

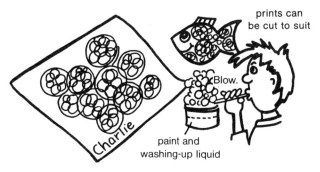

Copymasters
Use copymaster 84 (Air) to record this Area of Study. Go for a walk round school and see how many examples of trapped or moving air can be seen. Draw them in the boxes and write where they were spied. Write 'Trapped' or 'Moving' in the empty balloon and use a separate sheet to record examples of each.

 # METEOROLOGICAL SYMBOLS

Purpose
To show children how to understand and interpret the common meteorological symbols.

Outline activities
Watch videos of weather forecasts and note all the symbols used and the weather they represent. Using a chart of the British Isles and card symbols with Blu-Tack®, invent weather forecasts you would like. Watch the forecasts at the beginning of the day on TV and see if they were correct.

 # WEATHERING AND SOIL FORMATION

Purpose
To show that the weather affects materials and helps form soils.

Outline activities
a) Look round school for examples of weathering on buildings. Look for areas which are in the path of the wind, the rain and which are not sheltered. Note where moss, lichen and algae grow as these contribute to the breakdown of rocks. Look for crumbling surfaces on bricks, walls, trees. Note wind-bent trees, soil eroded by heavy rain or waterway or wind.

b) Collect different types of rocks to show the children and show them how water and wind break down rocks to produce grit. You can hold a piece of soft rock such as limestone under a jet of water and watch how small pieces will collect in the washings.

c) Look at local soil and see what it is made of. Soil is made of rock and plant and animal material in various quantities. Take soil from three different places in school, put a handful in a screw top jar, fill with water, put the lid on and shake vigorously. Leave to settle. After a period the materials in the soil will separate, leaving the rock at the bottom and light plant and animal remains at the top. You should be able to see some differences in make up quite clearly. Discuss the merits of different soils at a very simple level.

Record pictorially, or use photographs of the soil in the jars and the site of its origin. Take out the different materials and leave to dry so that you can examine them closely. Don't forget that water is also part of soil.

Attainment target 10: Forces

Pupils should develop their knowledge and understanding of forces; their nature, significance and effects on the movement of objects.

Statements of attainment

Level 3

Pupils should:

- understand that when things are changed in shape, begin to move or stop moving, forces are acting on them.
- understand the factors which cause objects to float or sink in water.

Area of study 1

FLOATING AND SINKING

C85

Purpose
To help the children to understand the factors which cause objects to float or sink in water.

Materials needed
Plastic bottles, drinks can, plastic tube, sponge, Plasticine®, stone, apple, orange, pieces of wood, egg, coins, polystyrene, seeds, erasers, candle, pumice stone, marbles or paper clips, straws, glass.

Activity 1: Explore floating and sinking
Test to see which of the objects collected float and which sink. Sort the material into two groups.

Activity 2
Choose several solid objects. Make sure they are not hollow. The children can guess which ones will float then test to see if they were right. Objects could include a stone, an apple, an orange, a piece of wood, a screw, an egg, coins, seeds, an eraser, a pumice stone.

Activity 3: Observe how wood floats
Try a range of different woods such as cork, mahogany, maple, ebony. A timber-yard may supply off-cuts of different rare types. Place the different woods on the water and see how they float.

Activity 4: Air helps things to float
Place a dry sponge on the surface of water and observe how it floats.
Now squeeze the air out of the sponge and wet it

thoroughly. Place it on the surface of the water again and see how it floats this time.

Place a drinks can on the water and it will float. Now fill the can with water and see if it will still float.

An empty bottle with a screw cap will float. But fill it with water and it will sink. To make the bottle float again place one end of a plastic tube into the neck of the bottle and blow air in from the other end. The bottle will float to the top because the air pushed the water out.

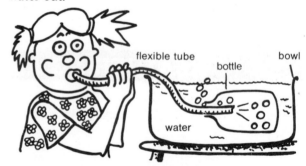

flexible tube   bottle   bowl

water

Activity 5: Shape helps things to float
Take a lump of Plasticine®, roll it into a ball and place it on the water. It will sink to the bottom. Try making different shapes with the Plasticine®, including a shallow boat and a boat with deep sides. Which floats best?

The shape of the object controls the amount of water that it pushes out of the way or displaces. If the amount of water that is displaced weighs more than the object then it will float and vice versa.

102

Test this by loading the Plasticine® boat with a cargo of paper clips or marbles. Add one at a time and the boat will sit lower in the water until it finally sinks.

Ships may sink if they are overloaded, so all ships have a mark on the side. It indicates how long the ship can float in the water without sinking. Make some floats with drinking straws. First of all float the straws in water and mark the water line on them. Then try the floats in salt water, milk and cooking oil. Do the straws float higher or lower in the different liquids?

Copymasters

Use copymaster 85 (Floating and sinking) to record the floaters and sinkers.

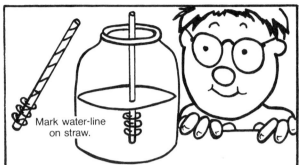

FORCES

Area of study 2

Purpose

To identify the forces which cause objects to change in shape, to begin to move or stop moving.

Outline activities

a) Solid pressure. Striking causes change. Strike cardboard boxes and press, pull and stretch Plasticine®.

b) Air pressure. Blow up balloons, explore the effect of moving air on sails, windmills and kites.

c) Water pressure. Play with jets of water. Find out about rivers and floods and water wheels.

d) Steam. Play with toy steam engines and make a steam-powered wheel (see below).

e) Gravity. Drop objects! Play with toy cars on slopes.

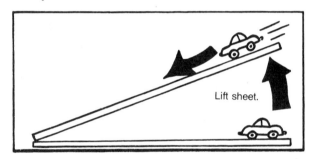

Lift sheet.

When the sheet is raised the car moves forward by the force of gravity and its own weight, without being pushed or pulled.

Steam-powered wheel

lid

hole

strong tin can

water boiling

foil wheel turned by force of jet of steam

safety goggles

heat source

Attainment target 11: Electricity and magnetism

Pupils should develop their knowledge and understanding of electric and electromagnetic effects in simple circuits, electric devices and domestic appliances.

Statements of attainment

Level **3**

Pupils should:

- know that some materials conduct electricity well while others do not.
- understand that a complete circuit is needed for an electrical device, such as a bulb or buzzer, to work.

Area of study 1

ELECTRICAL CIRCUITS

C86

Purpose

To show that a circuit is needed for an electrical device to work.

Materials needed

An assortment of small bulbs and batteries (use these combinations: 1.25 V bulb with a 1.5 V battery, 3.5 V bulb with a 4.5 V battery, 6 V bulb with a 6 V battery), lengths of thin insulated wire of different colours, bulb holders and wooden boards, scissors, small screwdrivers, crocodile clips or paper clips, small models of lighthouse or house.

Activity 1

Collect the equipment and let the children handle it and discuss freely. Examine the different pieces, the structure of the bulbs, the wire and the bulb holder.

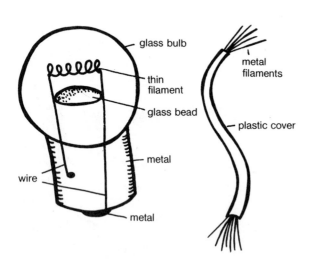

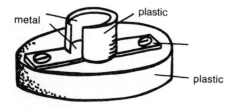

 Remind the children of the dangers of mains electricity. You can never do this too often. They should even be warned that the charge in a small battery should be treated with respect.

Activity 2

Show the children how to make a circuit to light the bulb. Allow them to try to construct a circuit themselves, in pairs. Ask them to get the materials needed themselves. The circuit needs to be constructed in a sequence so give them some practice in explaining to you and other children exactly how they made their circuit.

Activity 3

Set up several examples of different circuits as shown, some of which will work and some which will not, in order to make the point that there needs to be a continuous pathway for the electricity from the battery. If the pathway is complete then the bulb will light. The children will need a great deal of practice to understand this thoroughly.

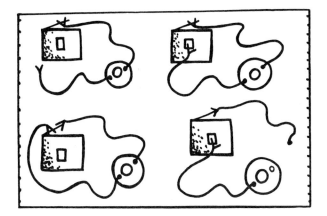

Tracing the path of the electricity with a finger and drawing the circuit helps. Encourage them to make big bold drawings to avoid confusion over joints.

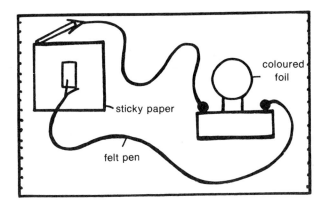

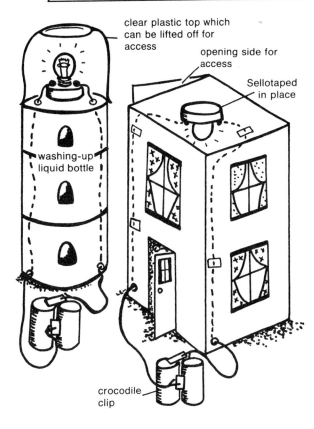

clear plastic top which can be lifted off for access

opening side for access

Sellotaped in place

washing-up liquid bottle

crocodile clip

Activity 4
If the bulb does not light, look for loose connections, dud bulbs and battery. Encourage the children to form a research routine to discover faults.

Activity 5: Light up!
Using a simple circuit put a light in a model house or lighthouse or on top of a model police car.

Copymasters
Use copymaster 86 (Circuits) to record this Area of Study. The children should first discuss the different examples with a partner and then make a guess as to the outcome. They can then try each out and see if their guess was correct. The complete circuits can then be marked on the sheet.

Area of study 2

CONDUCTORS AND INSULATORS

Purpose
To show that some materials conduct electricity while others do not.

Outline activities
Make a simple circuit and then introduce different materials into this circuit to see if the electricity will still flow. Keep checking that the original circuit is working and make two lists: Conductors and Insulators. Use materials such as fabric, wood, plastic, ceramic, paper, an apple, a stick of celery, various metals.

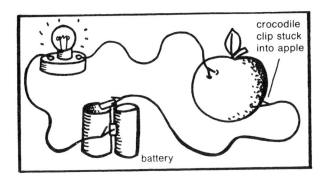

crocodile clip stuck into apple

battery

Attainment target 12: The scientific aspects of information technology including microelectronics

Pupils should develop their knowledge and understanding of information transfer and microelectronics.

Level 3

Statements of attainment

Pupils should:

- be able to store information using devices, for example, *a tape recorder, and a digital watch*.
- know that information can be stored electronically in a variety of ways, for example, *text, number, pictures and sound*.
- be able to retrieve and select text, number, sound or graphics stored on a computer.

Area of study 1

USING A TAPE RECORDER

Purpose
To show how to store information on a tape recorder.

Materials needed
Tape recorder, tape cassette.

Activity 1
Ask the children to bring in any of their own pre-recorded tapes of music and stories, or of family 'archive' material: baby's first words, Dad singing in the bath, etc. Many stories are now available on tape, e.g. the Narnia series by C.S. Lewis and many Roald Dahl stories. Play small selections to whet the appetite and give a purpose to the activity.

Activity 2
Show the children how the machine is made, i.e. look at the microphone, power source, cassette holder and the different buttons. It is better to work in small groups so that the children can handle the machine.

Warn about the dangers of wet hands near electrical appliances. Check school policy on children plugging in devices.

Activity 3
The tape recorder and many machines like it will only operate if the correct procedure is followed in the correct sequence so children need to learn this. There are many different types and makes and the range of functions varies but the basic procedure is the same for playing a tape:

a) Check power source is available, i.e. batteries or electrical mains supply and lead with plug.
b) Plug in and then switch on power supply. Note on/off switch at mains supply and on tape recorder if it has one.
c) Press EJECT to open cassette holder.

d) Select which side you want to play then load tape cassette into holder.
e) Check the tape is wound back to the beginning by pressing REWIND. Some recorders have an automatic stop when rewind is finished; if not press STOP.
f) Press PLAY.
g) Check volume as the tape plays and adjust if necessary.

Look at these functions also: PAUSE, FAST FORWARD and the counter if one is fitted.

Activity 4
Give the children plenty of practice at playing tapes themselves, then get groups to explain the procedure in the form of a poster with a picture sequence. Now for the acid test! Let groups swap posters and see if the procedure shown is correct.

Activity 5: Storing information (making a tape recording)
This skill will be useful to record work from other Attainment Targets.

Most tape recorders need PLAY to be pressed simultaneously with RECORD; some have a single function button. Follow the procedure outlined above to f) then record the item. Press STOP when the recording is over and REWIND to replay.

Activity 6
Let the children record each other speaking or singing. Telling jokes is good recording material!

Copymasters
Use copymaster 87 (Using a tape recorder) to record this Area of Study. Children are to look at the pictures and put them in the correct sequence by writing the numbers in the boxes at the bottom.

STORING AND RETRIEVING

Area of study 2

Purpose
To show children that information is stored electronically in a variety of ways and to show them how to store and retrieve it.

Outline activities
Look at the range of devices available in school as in Level 2 (see page 74). Let the children have as much access as possible to word processors, calculators, tape recorders, videos and a variety of software and tapes, to complement other areas of the curriculum. By this stage many children will have used computers and be familiar with the keyboard. Show them how to load software in the disc drive and how to select and retrieve the information stored therein.

Attainment target 13: Energy

Pupils should develop their knowledge and understanding of the nature of energy, its transfer and control.

They should develop their knowledge and understanding of the range of energy sources and the issues involved in their exploitation.

Level 3

Statements of attainment

Pupils should:

- understand, in qualitative terms, that models and machines need a source of energy in order to work.
- know that temperature is a measure of how hot (or cold) things are.
- be able to use simple sources (electric motors, rubber bands) and devices which transfer energy (gears, belts, levers).

TEMPERATURE AS A MEASURE

Area of study 1

C88

Purpose
To show that temperature is a measure of hot and cold.

Materials needed
Video of weather forecasts, selection of thermometers with degrees in Fahrenheit and Celsius, three bowls, water, paper, pens.

Activity 1
In order to know that temperature is a measure of how hot or cold things are, the children will not only have to see a thermometer working but also have experience of using one. The teacher's first job is to show the children how to use the instrument.

Put cold, warm and hot water in three separate bowls. Using a simple Celsius thermometer for each, rest it in the water to display the respective temperatures. Show the children how the thermometer is constructed and how to read the scale.

Activity 2
Watch videos of weather forecasts and pay particular attention to the temperatures. Show the children the two types of scale, Celsius and Fahrenheit, using actual thermometers, so that they can get an idea of

0°Celsius = 32°Fahrenheit
100°Celsius = 212°Fahrenheit

whether it will be hot or cold by looking at the temperature.

For example, −2° or −1 °C usually gives a frost
10 °C is chilly
20 °C is hot

Activity 3
Take the temperature outside in the playground every day for a week and record the results on a chart. Which were the warmest and coldest days? Discuss how to make this test fair.

107

Activity 4
Measure the children's body temperature. Use a variety of thermometer designs to show the wide range and different types of readings.

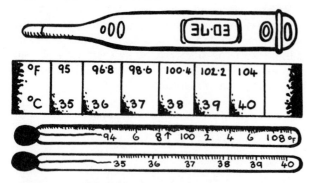

Make a bar chart to record the temperature of everyone in the class. Tell the children the normal temperature range of the human body and the variations which indicate illness. Is anyone in the class ill?

Activity 5
To give a great deal of practice in the significance of temperature conduct a temperature survey of school. Measure the temperature round the classroom, finding a sunny spot, a dark spot, a shady spot. Find the hottest place and put other positions in the classroom in a sequence according to the temperature. Put these temperatures and grades on card labels and stick them to the actual places round the room.

Take the temperature in the centre of the classroom daily at the same time and note on which day in the week the temperature is highest. Take the temperature in the same spot at different times to see if it varies in a day. Take the temperature round school, near doors, in the corridors, playground, garden, staffroom, kitchen, caretaker's room, head's room and each classroom.

Copymasters
Use copymaster 88 (Shall I play outside?) to record this Area of Study. The children colour in the mercury on the thermometer to represent the temperature shown and then draw themselves and their friends, appropriately dressed, playing outside. They should also draw in appropriate weather for the temperature.

 MODELS AND MACHINES

Area of study 2

Purpose
To show that models and machines need an energy source.

Outline activities
Ask the children to bring in a selection of toys that work. Play with them and try to find out what powers them: battery, mains electricity, springs, gears and levers, pulleys, rubber bands, etc. Make sets of things which are powered by the same source.

Look round school and see how many different machines you can find, e.g. photocopiers, spirit duplicators (hand and mains), cleaning machines, computers, typewriters, hydraulic arms on doors, locks.

 SIMPLE POWER SOURCES

Area of study 3

Purpose
To use a simple power source.

Outline activities
Use the toys collected for the preceding Area of Study.

Study how the various items work. Try to identify devices which transfer energy, such as levers, gears, belts, strings.

| clockwork | spring | radio-controlled | battery |

Attainment target 14: Sound and music

Pupils should develop their knowledge and understanding of the properties, transmission and absorption of sound.

Level 3	**Statements of attainment**

Pupils should:

- know that sounds are produced by vibrating objects and can travel through different materials.
- be able to give a simple explanation of the way in which sound is generated and can travel through different materials.

 Area of study 1

SOUNDS AND MATERIALS

 C89

Purpose
To show that sounds are produced by vibrating objects and can travel through different materials.

Materials needed
Tuning forks, large tin or bowl, plastic sheet or bag, small pieces of paper, spoon, tray, glass, tin foil, cotton, sugar, ruler, paper and comb, rubber bands, shoe box, spoons and string, glass jar, cotton wool, alarm clock, wood shavings, sand, Plasticine®, newspaper, thick woolly jumper.

Activity 1
It is difficult for many children to understand that vibrations are associated with sound, but most of them will appreciate that there has been some form of movement in the apparatus. Let the children watch and feel the vibration of the guitar, piano or cymbals. Let them feel the edge of the cymbals when they have been crashed together. Feel a record player or radio case when it is playing loudly and you will feel a vibration. (It is more difficult to appreciate the vibration of a wind instrument.)

Activity 2
Use a tuning fork and tap the two prongs on the edge of the table and listen to the sound. To see the vibrations, place the tuning fork's tip on the surface of a bowl of water and the water will ripple.

Activity 3
Cut along one side and the bottom of a plastic bag. Spread it tightly over the top of a big tin or bowl and secure it with a rubber band to make a drum.

Tear up paper into small pieces and put them on top of the drum. Tap the drum with a spoon and the paper will jump about.

Activity 4
To show that sound travels through air, hold a baking tray close to the drum and sprinkle sugar on top of the plastic sheet. Bang the tray hard with a spoon and you will see the sugar jump.

Activity 5
Another way to see vibrations of sound is to take an old wine glass, a piece of cotton and a ball of tin foil. Fix the cotton to the foil. Hold up the thread so that the foil ball just hangs against the edge of the glass, then tap the glass gently with a pencil and the ball will jump away (see overleaf for illustration).

Activity 6: Noisy ruler

Hold the end of a ruler firmly down on the edge of a table, pull the other end down and then let go. Try it with the ruler pulled out to different lengths.

Activity 7

Make a comb and paper kazoo and feel the vibrations on the lips.

Activity 8: Rubber band guitar

Stretch several rubber bands of different thickness across a shoe box. Refine this with a lid and a sound hole.

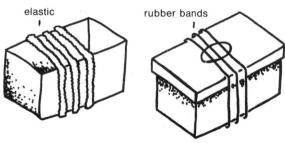

Vibrations make the air around them move and the air carries the sound to the ear. Will sound travel through materials? Find out by experimenting.

Activity 9

Children can test sound travelling through air, solids and liquids.

Listen to a pencil tapping on a table with ears above the table then on it. Listen to a coin tapping a metal pipe, first from above it then with an ear touching the pipe. Make noises underwater in the water tray and listen to the sound with the ears against the tray. Try banging a wall while the children stand with their ears pressed against the bricks at the other side. Tap the floor while the children lie with their ears pressed against the ground. Jangle spoons tied to a string and hold the end of the string to the ear.

Tap the railings outside school and see how far the sound will travel along them.

Activity 10: Muffling sound

Do some materials not let sound through? Turn on a radio and put it in a shoe box. Can you still hear it? How well? Now line the box with polystyrene tiles. Does this affect the sound? Listen to a watch through a jam jar, then stuff a duster into the jam jar. How is the sound affected?

Copymasters

Use copymaster 89 (Sounds and materials) to test which materials let sound pass through best. Children take a clock with a loud tick and wrap it up in a plastic bag to protect it and then place it in different materials. You will need three boxes to put the clock and the materials in: made of cardboard, tin and wood. Place the clock in one of the boxes and surround it with each of the materials suggested on the copymaster in turn.

EXPLAINING ABOUT SOUND

Area of study 2

Purpose

To give the children practice in putting forward an explanation of how sound is made and how it travels through some materials.

Outline activities

Children can discuss the findings of Area of Study 1. This can be recorded on audio or video tape, in writing, as a strip cartoon or as a live demonstration to the rest of the class.

Attainment target 15: Using light and electromagnetic radiation

Pupils should develop their knowledge and understanding of the properties and behaviour of light and electromagnetic waves.

 Level 3

Statements of attainment

Pupils should:

- know that light can be made to change direction and shiny surfaces can form images.
- be able to give an account of an investigation with mirrors.

Area of study 1

LIGHT CHANGES DIRECTION

 C90

Purpose
To show that light can be made to change direction and shiny surfaces can form images.

Materials needed
A selection of mirrors, several small rectangular hand mirrors, torches, a collection of shiny things.

Activity 1: Play with light beams
In a darkened room use several torches to make long beams. Notice how the beams are straight as light moves in straight lines.

Light can be made to change direction by reflecting it off a shiny surface such as a mirror.

Activity 2: Look round corners
Stand a child behind a corner with a mirror to look round the corner with. Does it have to be held round the corner to show what is there?

Activity 3
Get the children to use mirrors to look over their shoulders, above the head and below, but without moving the head.

Activity 4: Play with sunbeams
On a sunny day reflect the light from the window off a mirror on to the wall.

Activity 5: Chase sunbeams
Reflect the light from the Sun on to a wall, using a hand mirror. Get the children to play with a partner and try to catch each other's beam. Try tracing the lines of the bricks with the beam.

Activity 6: Watching light turn
Set up the apparatus as shown below. Notice how the light comes from the hole in a straight line and is reflected off the mirror in a straight line aswell.

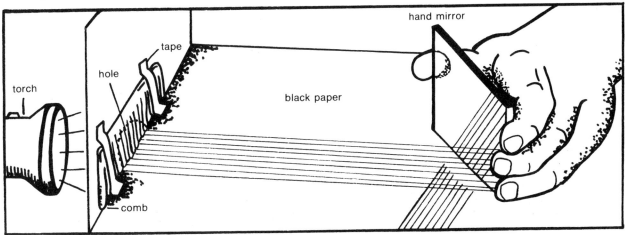

111

Activity 7: Look in a mirror

Let the children look at themselves in large mirrors and try touching their noses, eyes, ears while looking at the reflection. The mirror reverses the image of the child. Let them play at mirror moving with a partner to get a feel of this reversal.

Activity 8: More images

Play with pairs of taped mirrors to get more than one reflection. Make a kaleidoscope.

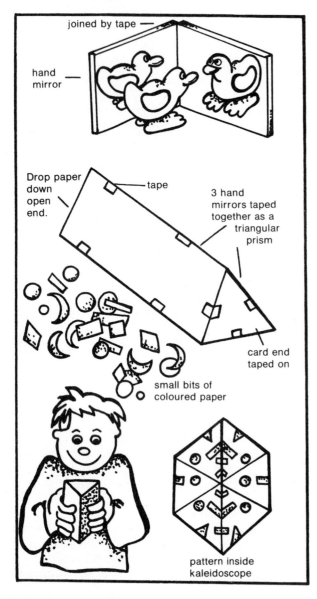

Activity 9

Hold two mirrors opposite each other with a small object between them to get an endless line of reflections.

Activity 10: Try mirror writing

Put a sheet of paper in front of a mirror and try writing while looking in the mirror. The resulting script is reversed like the child's own reflected image. This can be used as secret writing; a mirror is needed to decipher it.

Activity 11: Look at symmetry

If an object is symmetrical, the shape of the object will appear unchanged when a mirror is placed along the axis of symmetry. This is because the reflection will be the same shape as the half which is hidden. Test out several objects and pictures to see if they are symmetrical.

Activity 12: Look for shiny objects

Make a collection of shiny objects, such as an apple, a glass, a bottle, spoons, a kettle, a shaving mirror, a balloon, a snooker ball, shiny shoes, wellies, beads, sequins, foil, pottery, Christmas decorations. Look into puddles, a bowl of water, soap bubbles. Talk about the reflections seen in these things. Ask questions such as: Is the reflection like the object? Is it fatter or thinner? Is it back to front or upside down? Does the object look nearer or farther away than you expected? What shape are the shiny things which give a distorted image?

Make sets of these things according to how they reflect objects: true, fatter, thinner, reversed, etc. You can talk about concave and convex surfaces.

Copymasters

Use copymaster 90 (Using mirrors) to record this Area of Study. Each child will need two copies of the sheet. On the first, the children try to make the drawings symmetrical, relying on their eye alone. On the second sheet they can use a hand mirror held against the line of symmetry so that they can see the exact reflected image which they can then attempt to draw.

REPORTING

C90

Purpose
To help the children give an account of an investigation with mirrors.

Outline activities
Copymaster 90 can be used as a basis for the children to give an account of an investigation with mirrors. This can be reported in writing, or on tape recorder or orally to the group or class. Encourage them to report their actions and findings in sequence.

Attainment target 16: The Earth in space

Pupils should develop their knowledge and understanding of the relative positions and movement of the Earth, Moon, Sun and solar system within the universe.

Level 3

Statements of attainment

Pupils should:

● know that the inclination of the Sun in the sky changes during the year.
● be able to measure time with a sundial.

MAKING A SUNDIAL

C91

Purpose
To be able to measure time with a sundial.

Materials needed
Pictures and photos of sundials, stick, pebbles, torch, candlestick, paper, pencil.

Activity 1
Show the children pictures and photographs of sundials, or if there is one in a nearby park, go and see it, preferably on a sunny day.

There are two types of sundial, free-standing types in parks and gardens and the wall-mounted type usually found on the walls of old houses and churches.

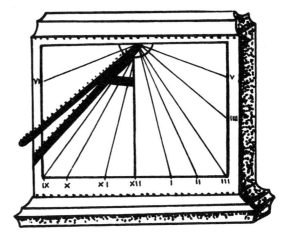

The sundial, as its name suggests, tells the time using the Sun. The pointer makes a shadow when the Sun shines and the instrument is so designed that the shadow falls on the same spot at the same time each day. See if the children notice that the numbers on the sundial are not the same and are not in the same positions as a more familiar clock face.

Activity 2
Make a simple sundial by pushing a stick into the lawn and use it during the course of one day to mark the hours. At nine o'clock in the morning, place a stone at the end of the shadow and mark this stone with a 9. Do this each hour throughout the day until home time. Provided the apparatus is not moved it will be possible to tell the time reasonably accurately whenever the Sun shines. If the shadow falls half way between the stones it is obviously half past the hour.

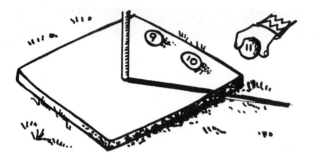

marking off the hours as before. This model can be taken in at night. Remember to site it in a sunny position.

Copymasters

Use copymaster 91 (Making a sundial) to record this Area of Study. The children can draw a picture of their finished sundial, whatever the design, and write an account of how they made it and how to use it.

Alternatively, fix a piece of dowel to the centre of a large piece of wood and use this as the sundial,

Area of study 2 — THE INCLINATION OF THE SUN

Purpose

To show the children that the inclination of the Sun in the sky changes during the year.

Outline activities

This activity is a long-term project which can take a whole year and this alone will help broaden the children's concept of time. They should be given opportunity to measure shadows of the same things in the same position at different times of the year, but at the same time of day.

In order to do this, find a place in school which is sunny but has little traffic, and an object which casts a conveniently sized shadow, like a skittle. Fix a piece of paper to the site and mark the shadow, noting the exact position. Store carefully and repeat at monthly intervals. The shadows' length will vary most between winter and summer.

Explain that the Earth rotates on an axis and that the curvature of the Earth's surface means that the Sun appears lower or higher in the sky according to the time of the year. The relationship between the length of shadow and the inclination of the Sun can be shown using a torch in a darkened room. When the torch is lower, the shadows are longer and vice versa.

Key Stage One AT1
Levels one & two

Name

Year/Class

A record of the number of experiences of AT1 processes.

👁	👤	?	🔍	📏	🗒	📖	💡

Comments

Key Stage One AT1
Level three

Name / **Year/Class**

A record of the number of experiences of AT1 processes.

H	🔍	⚖	⏱	🥤	📖	📊	🌀	1.2.3.4.

Comments

Key Stage One

Name												

Level   **Year/Class**

AT		Area of Study 1				Area of Study 2				Area of Study 3		
		a	b	c		a	b	c		a	b	c

Comments